I0442598

THIS BOOK BELONGS TO:

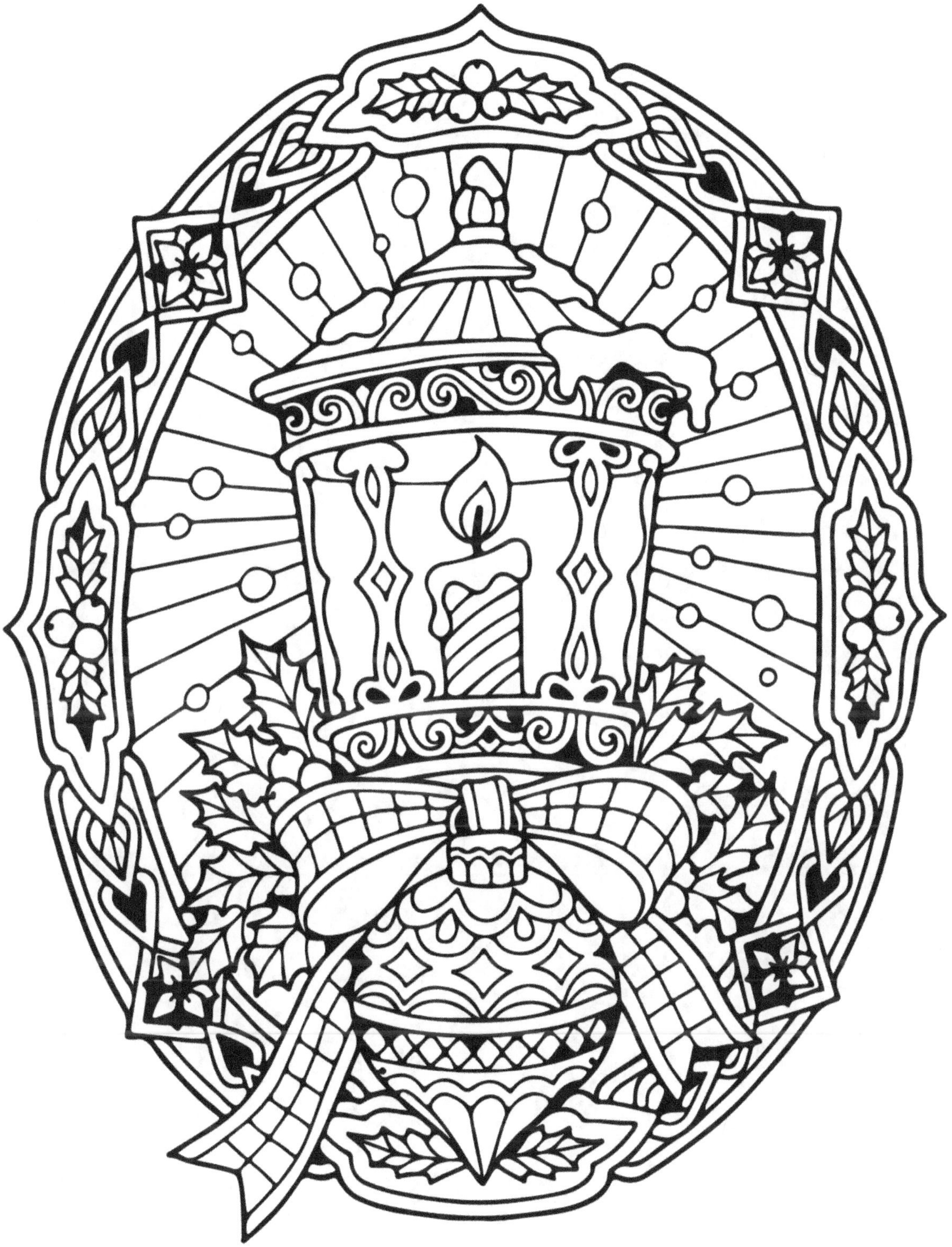

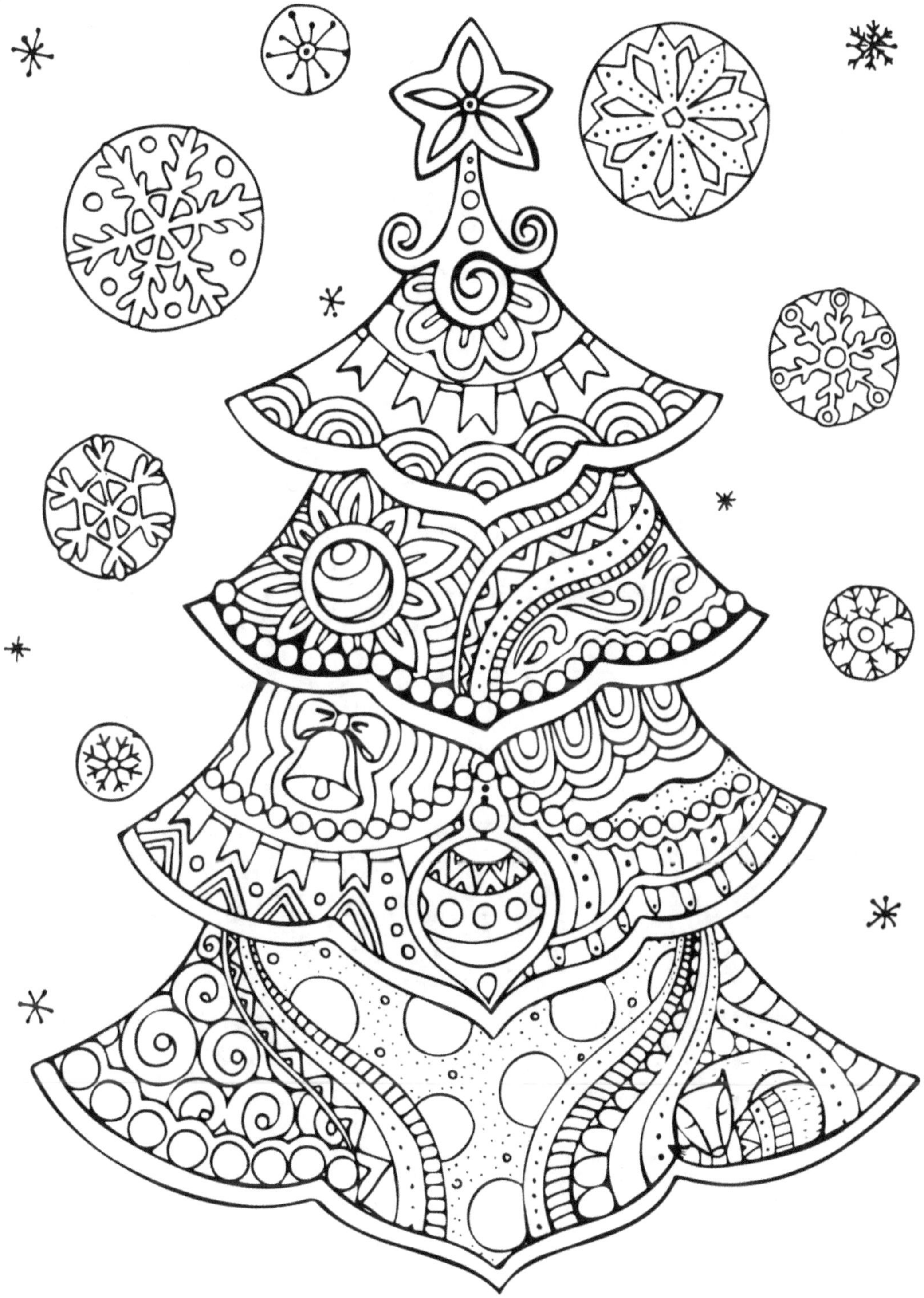

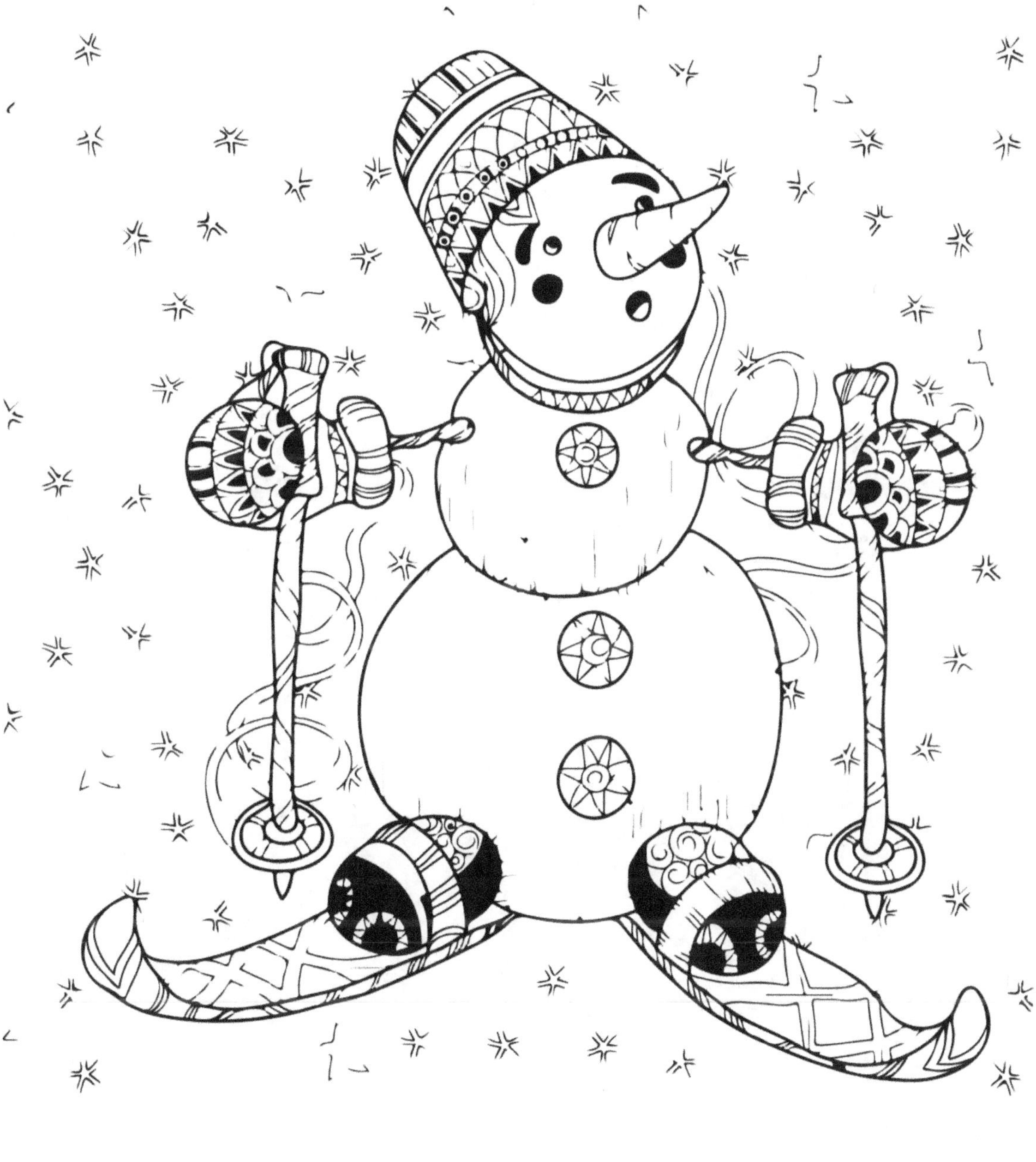

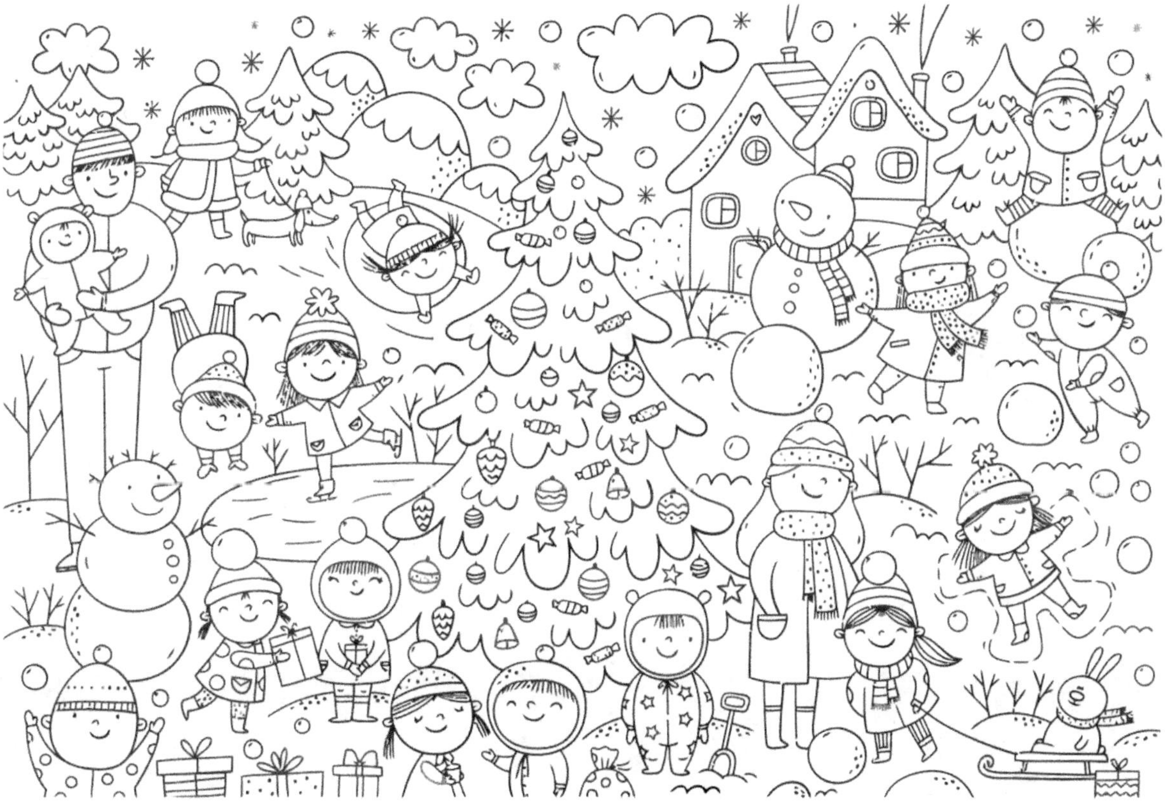

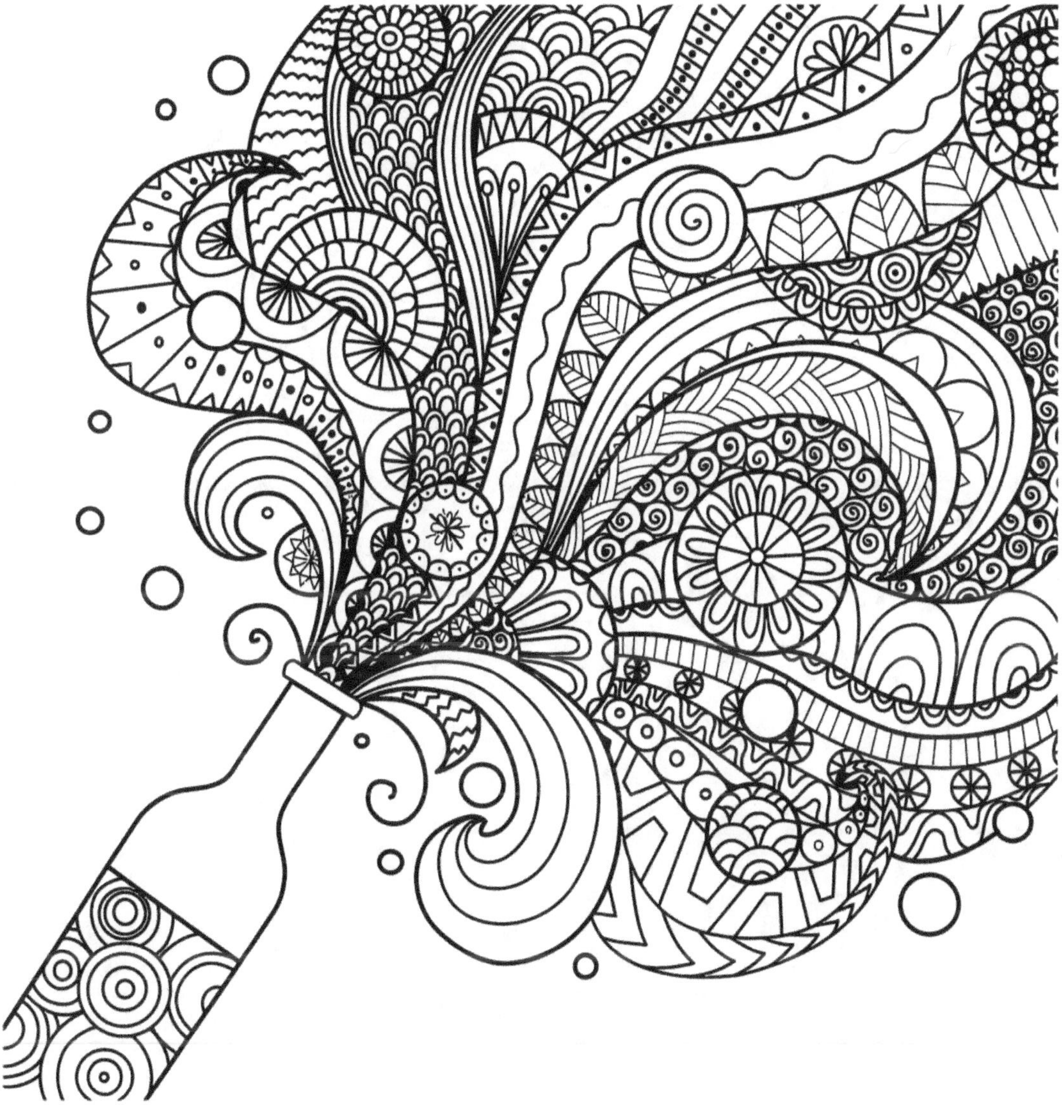

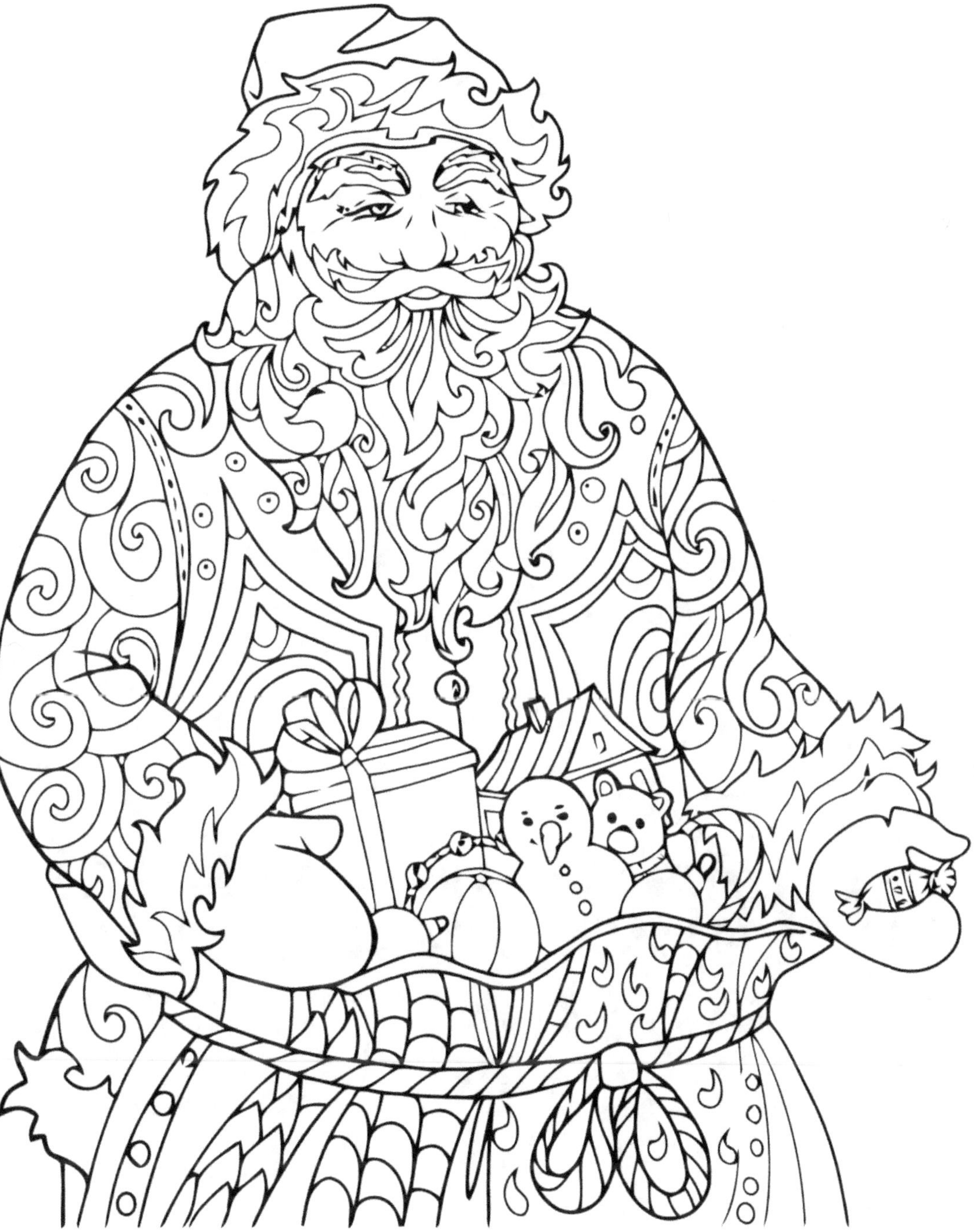

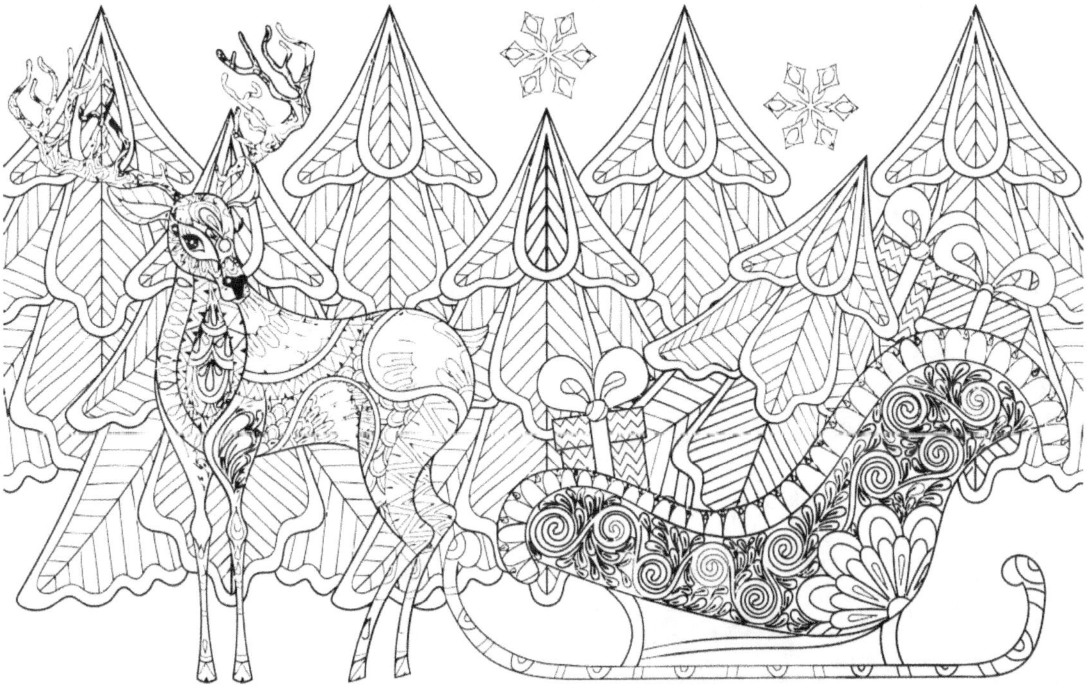

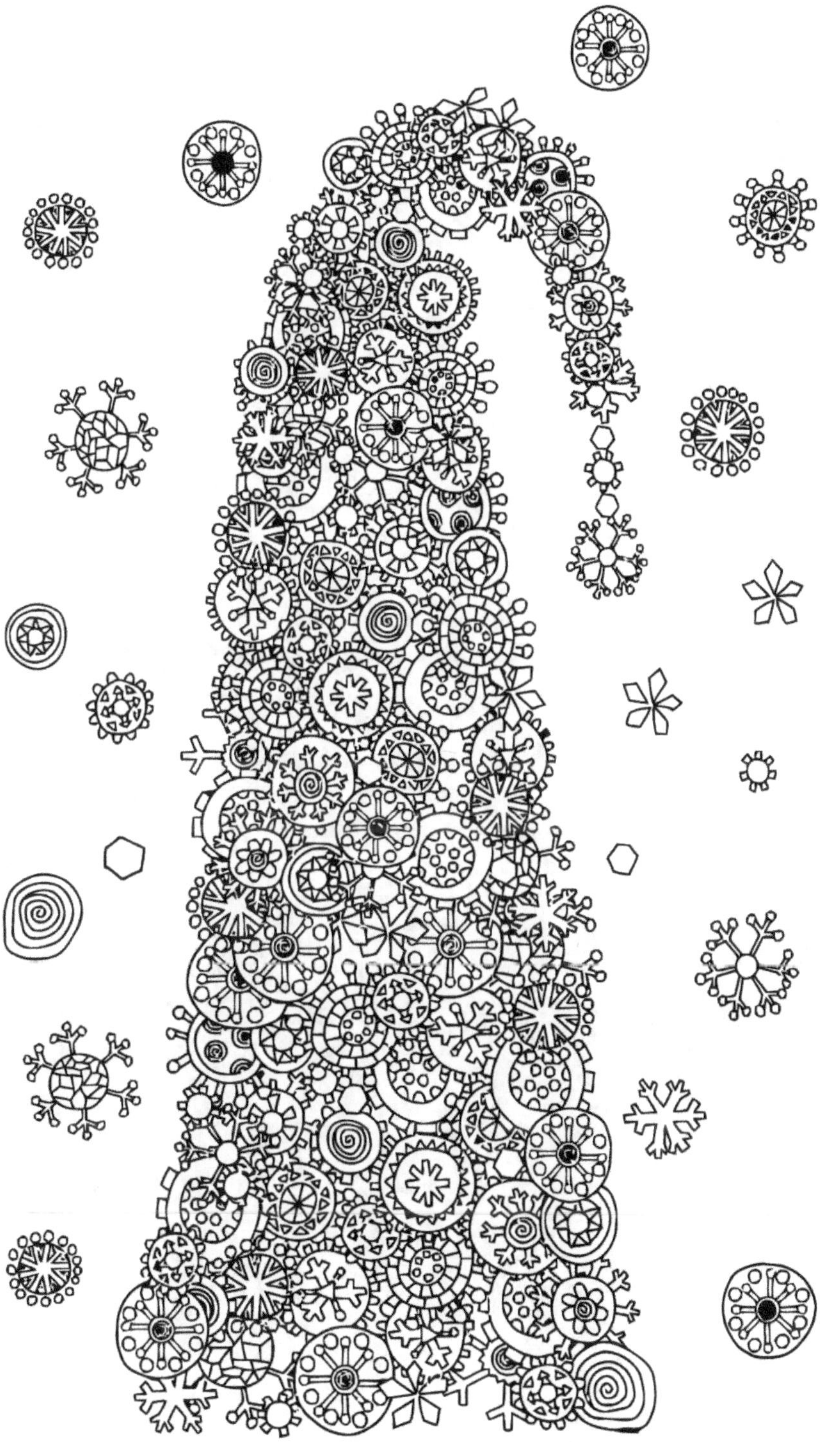

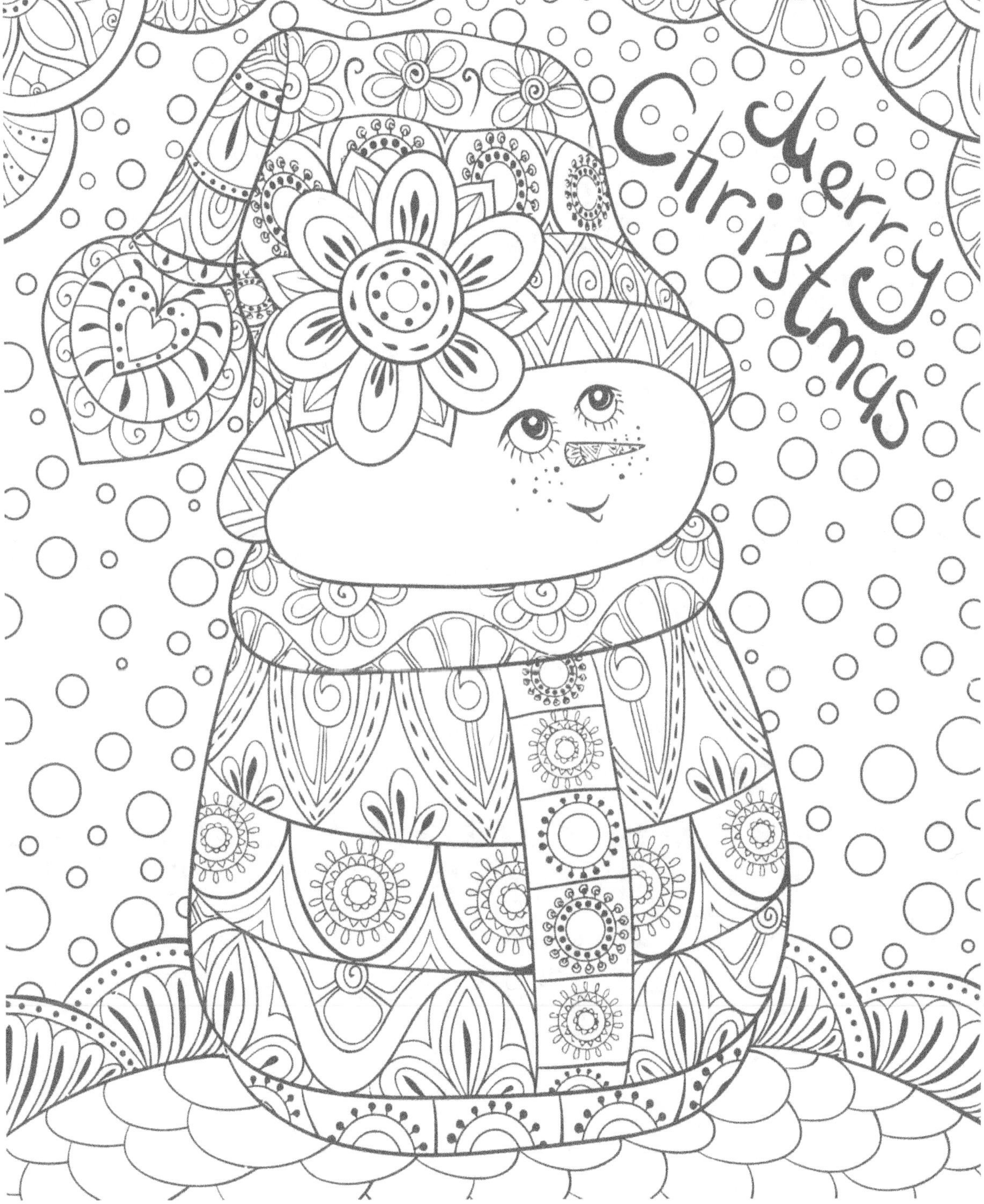
Merry Christmas

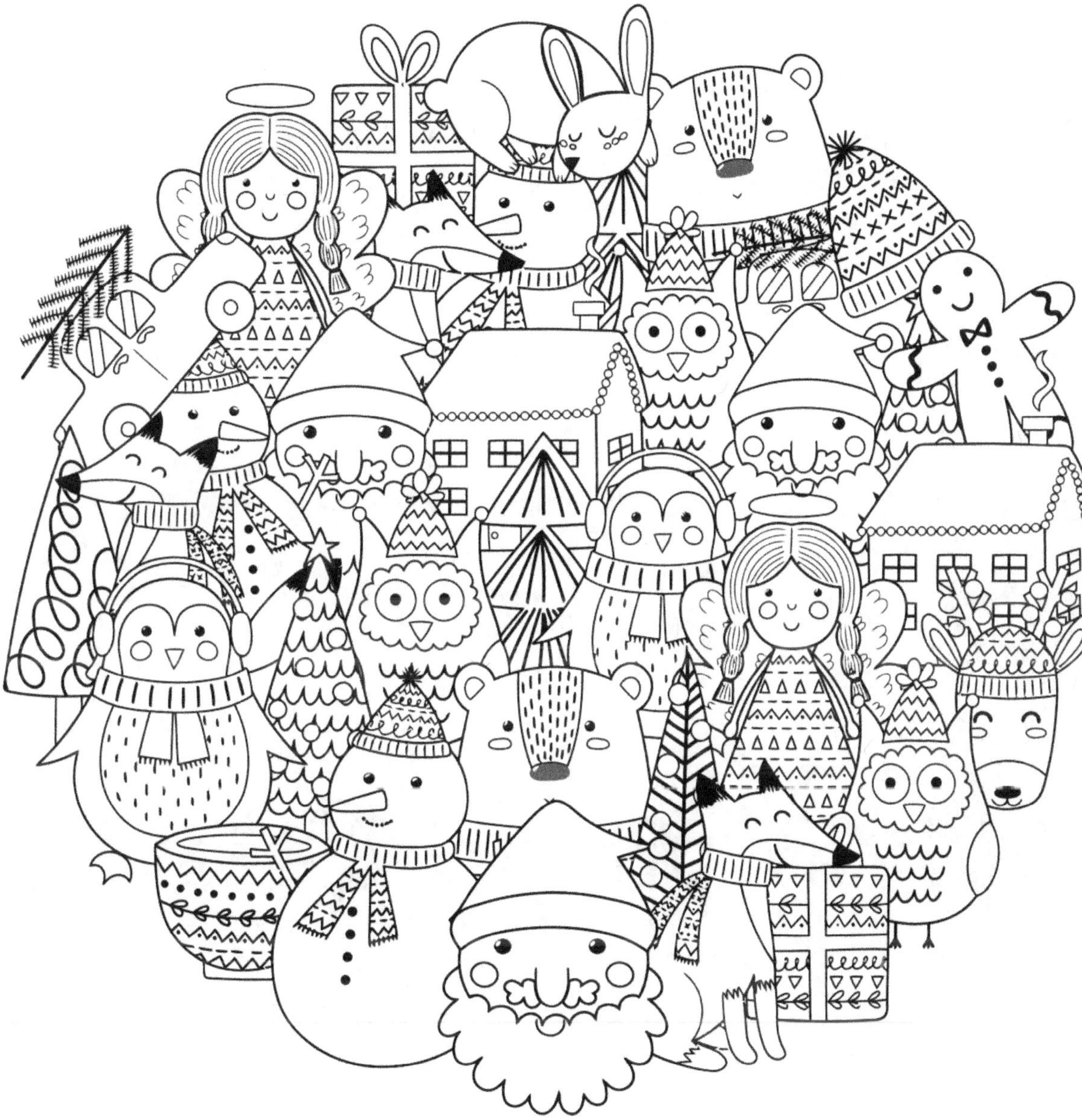

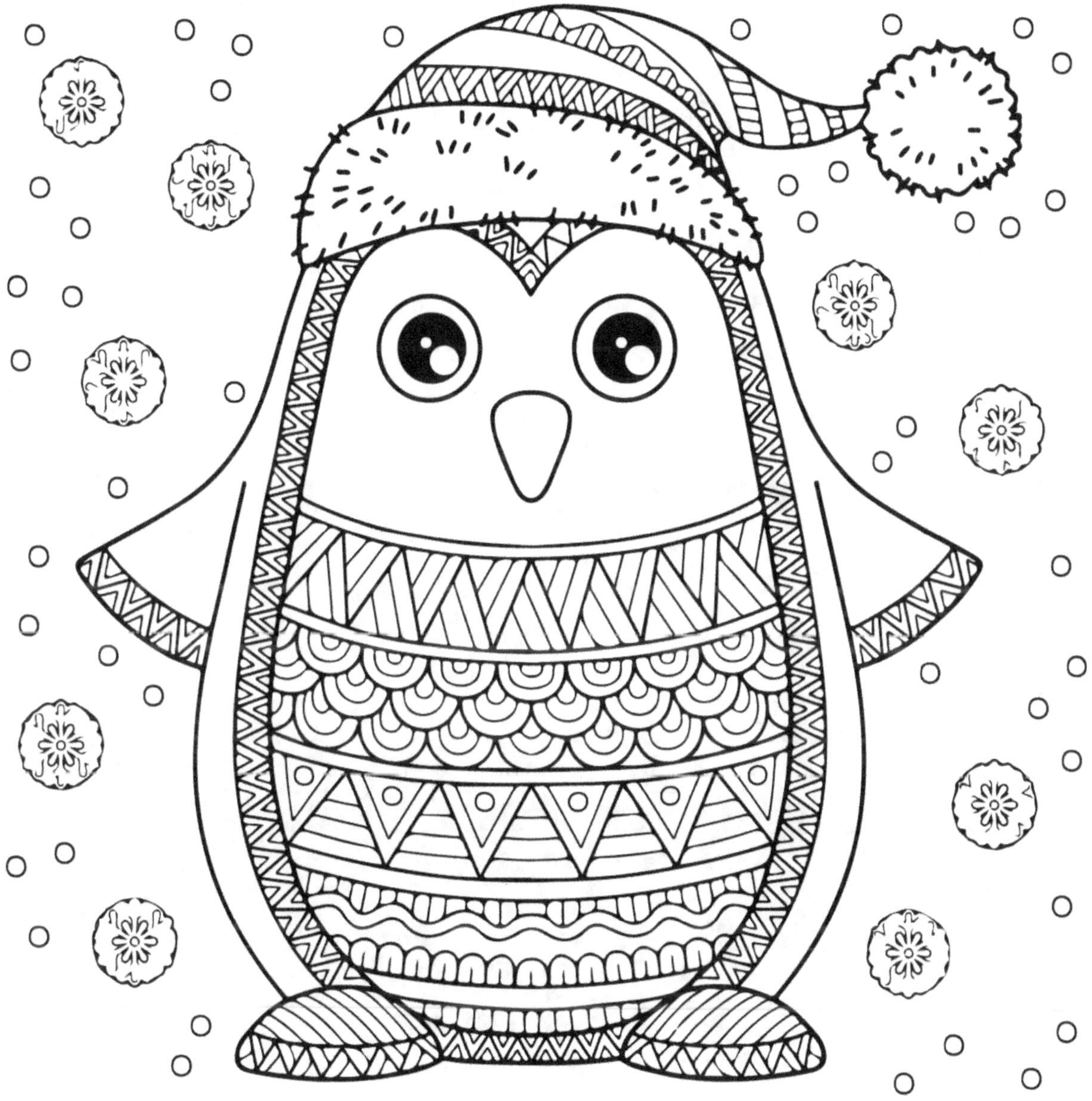

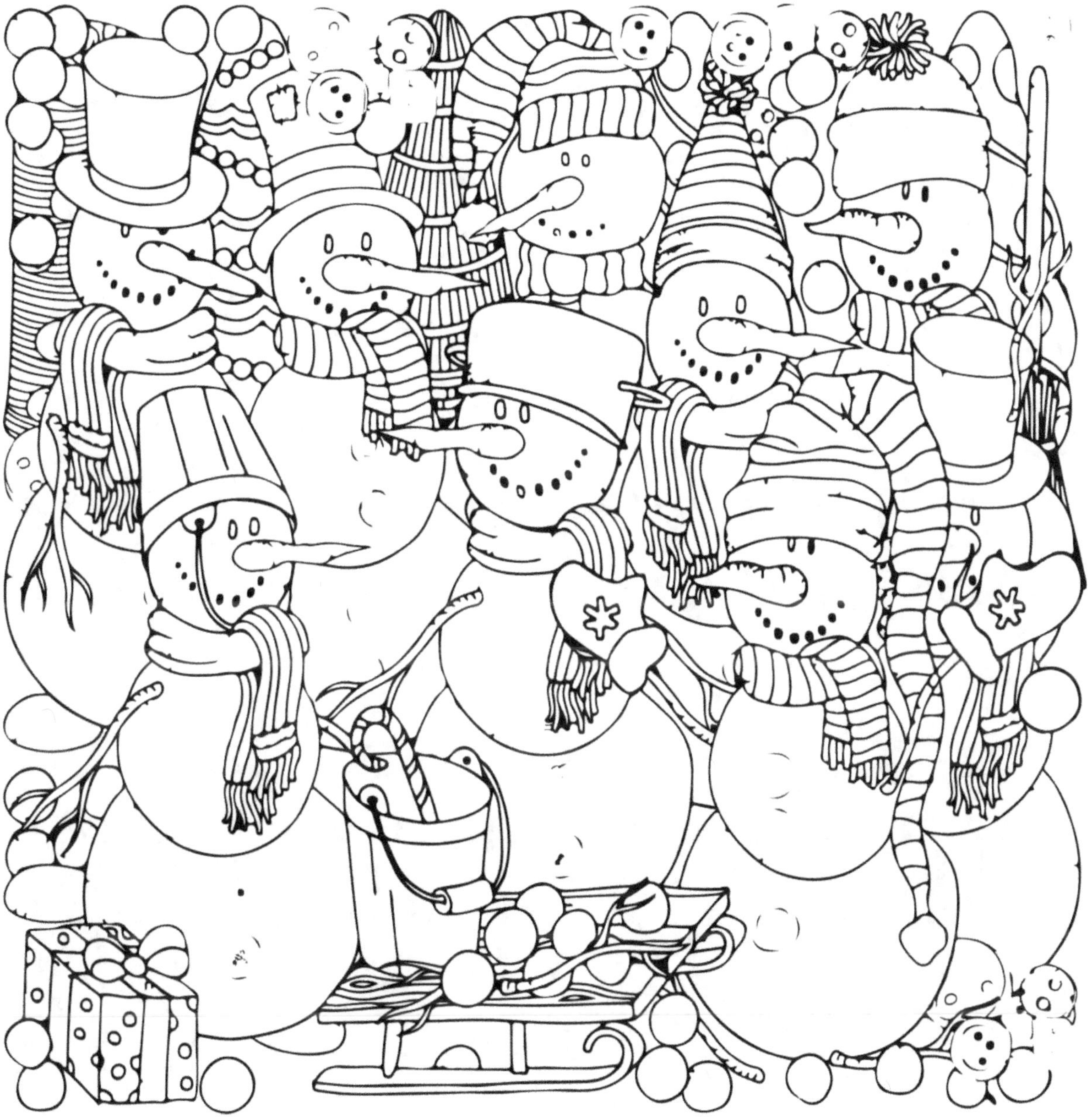

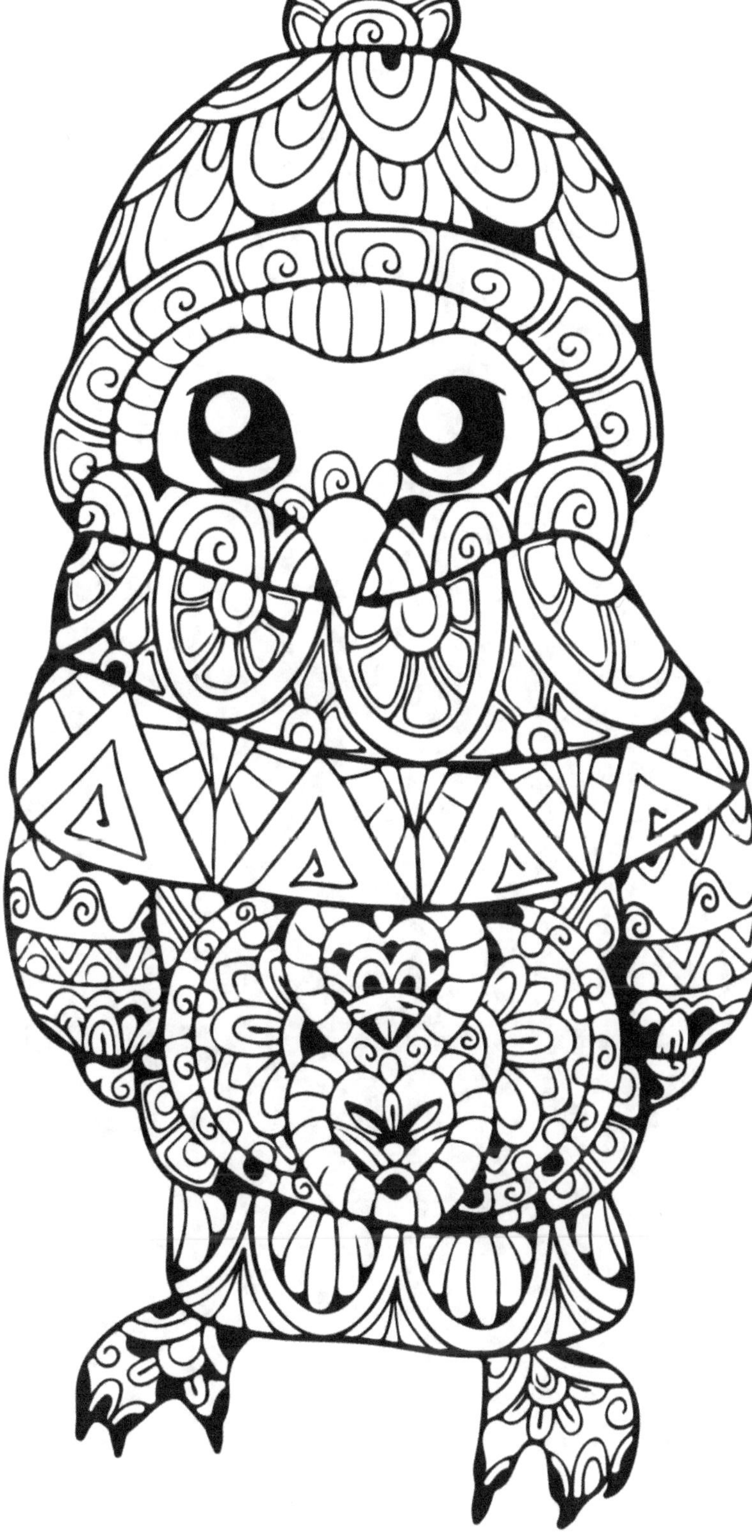

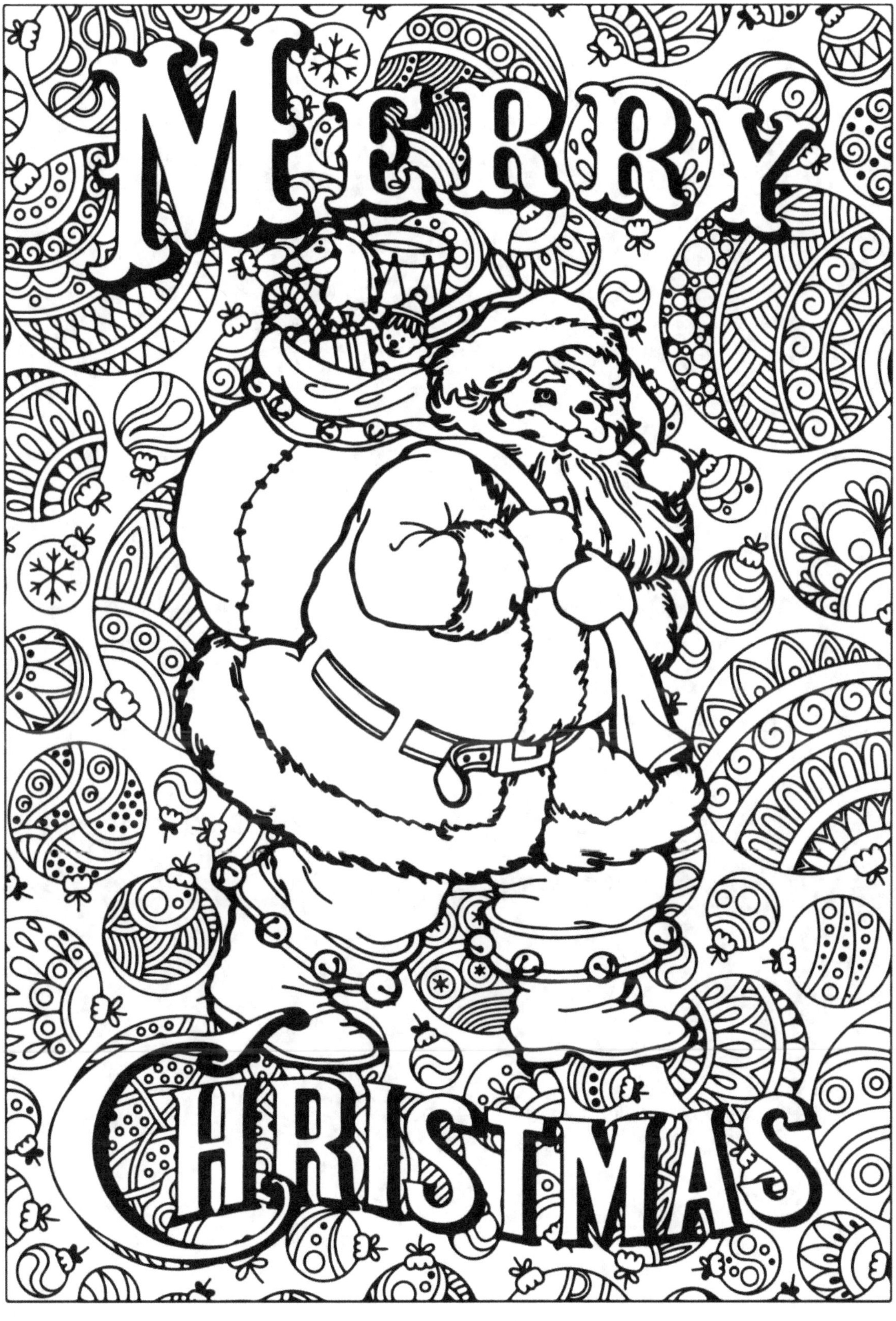
MERRY
CHRISTMAS

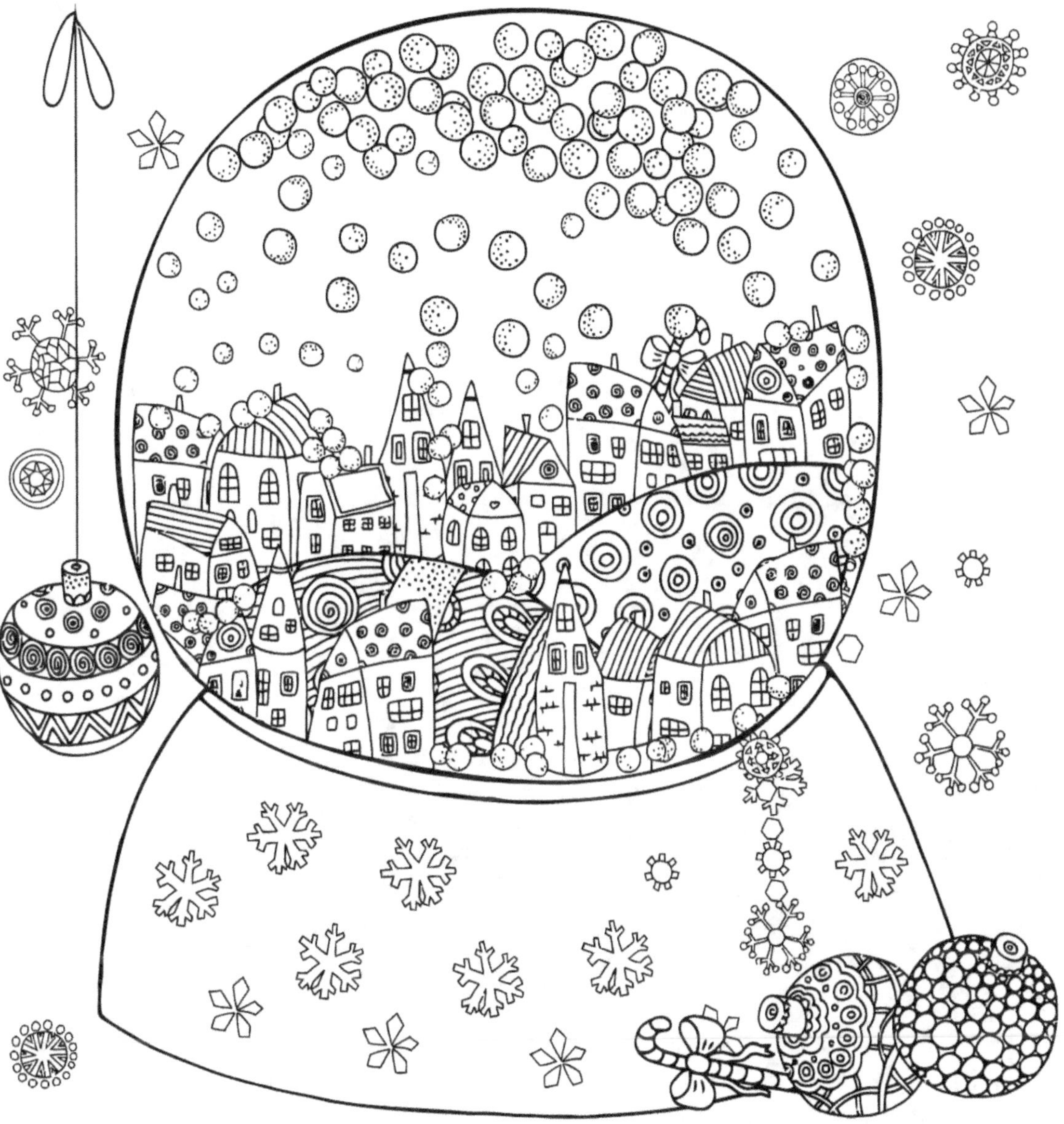

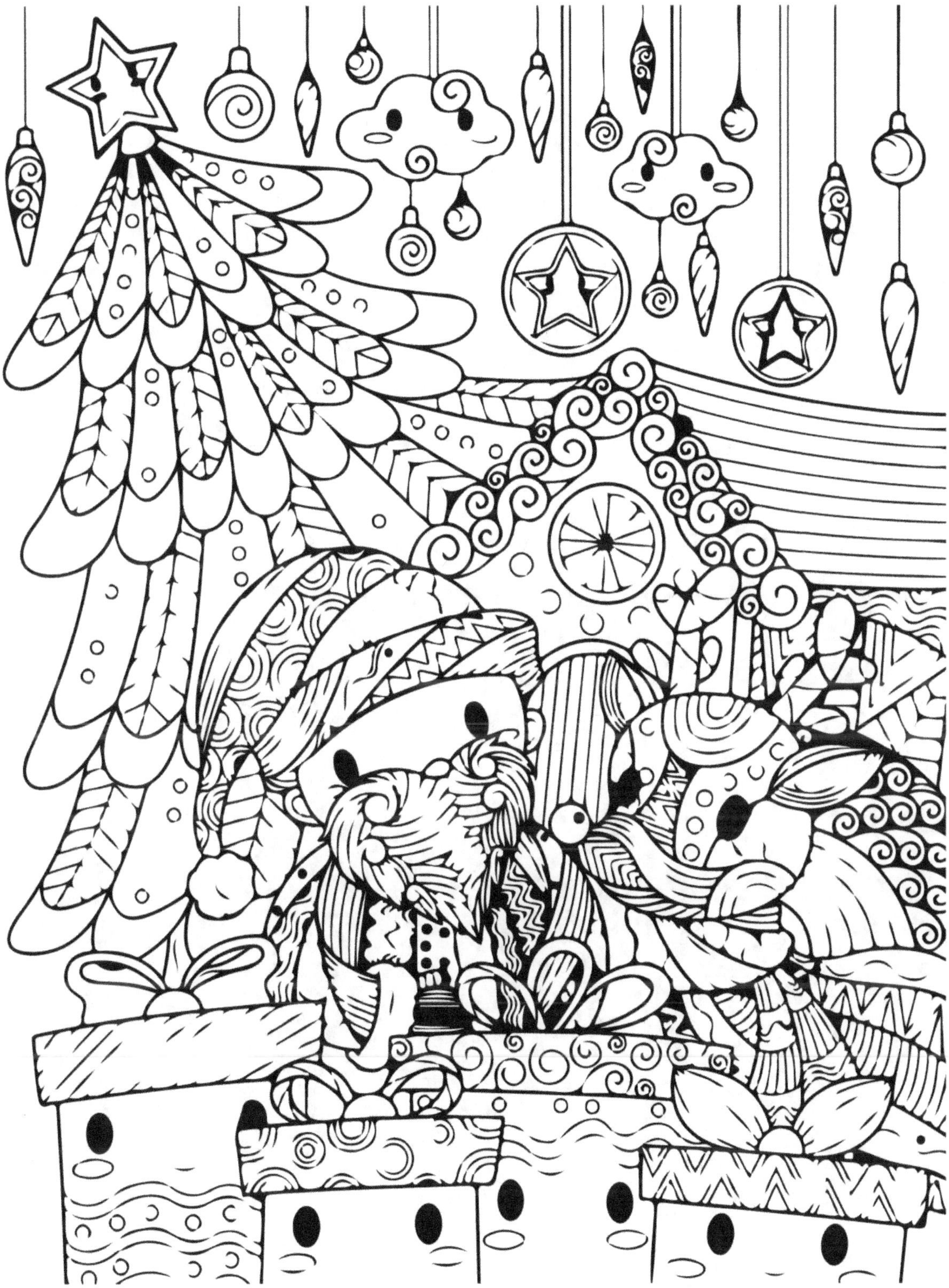

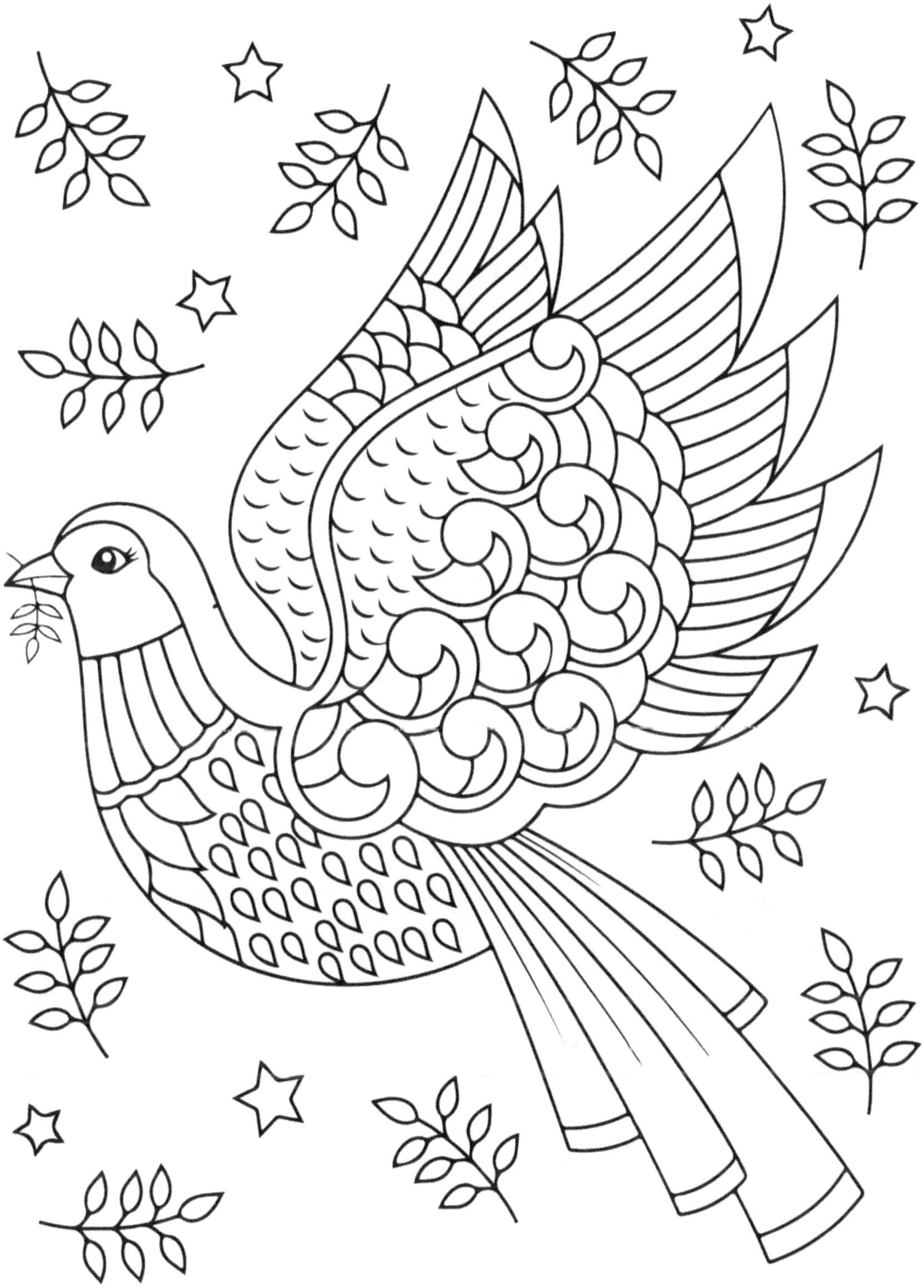

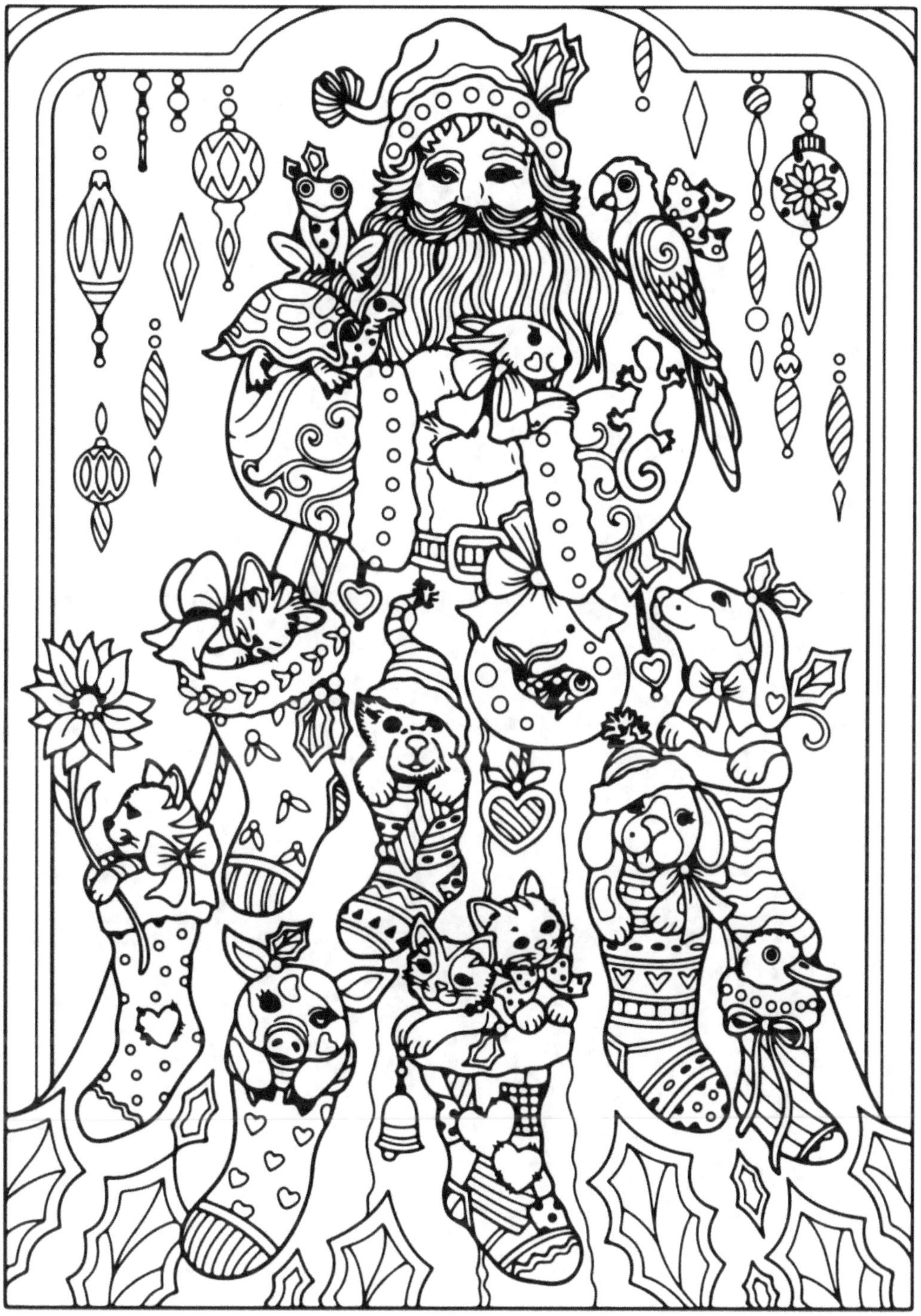

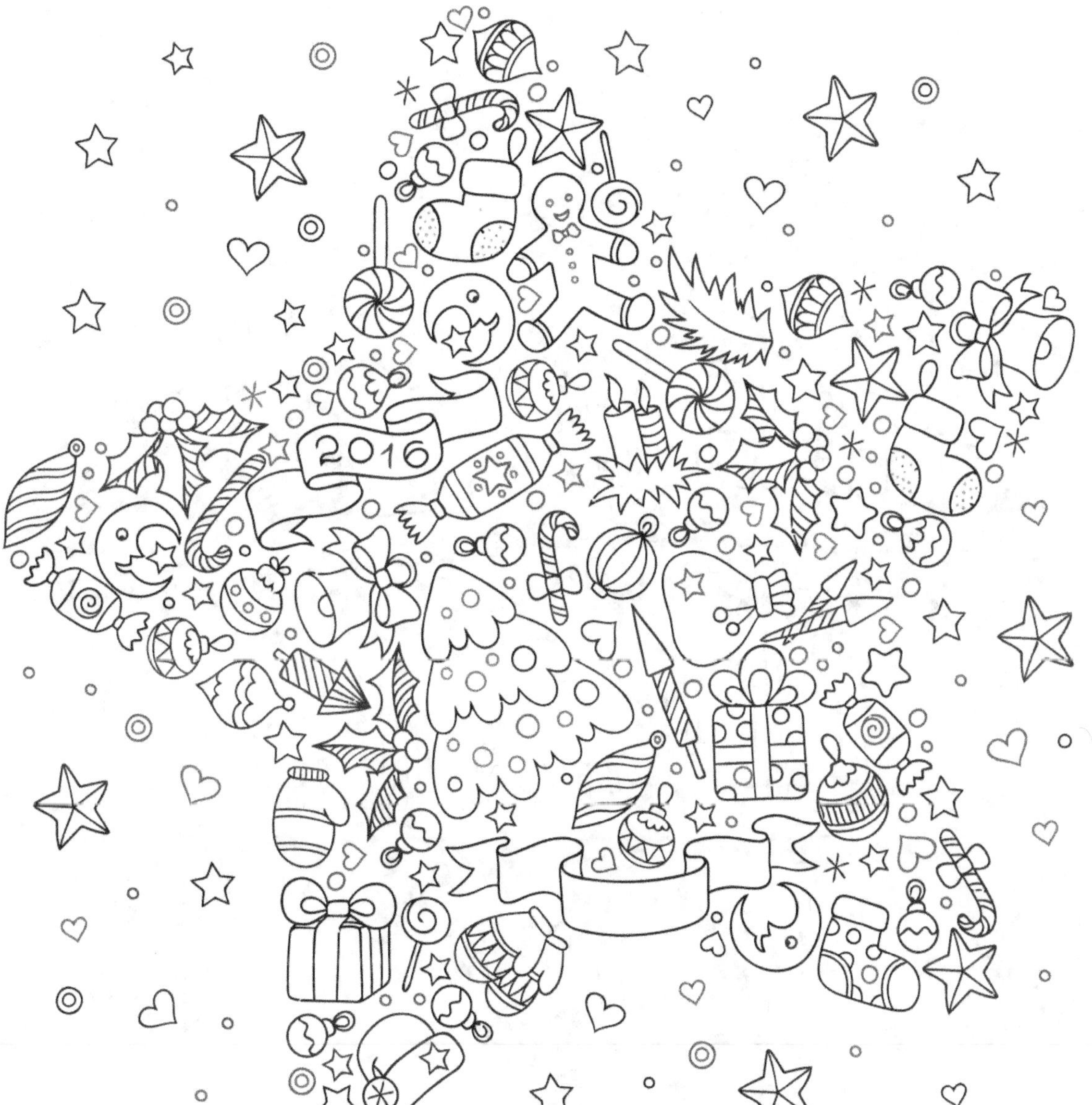
2016

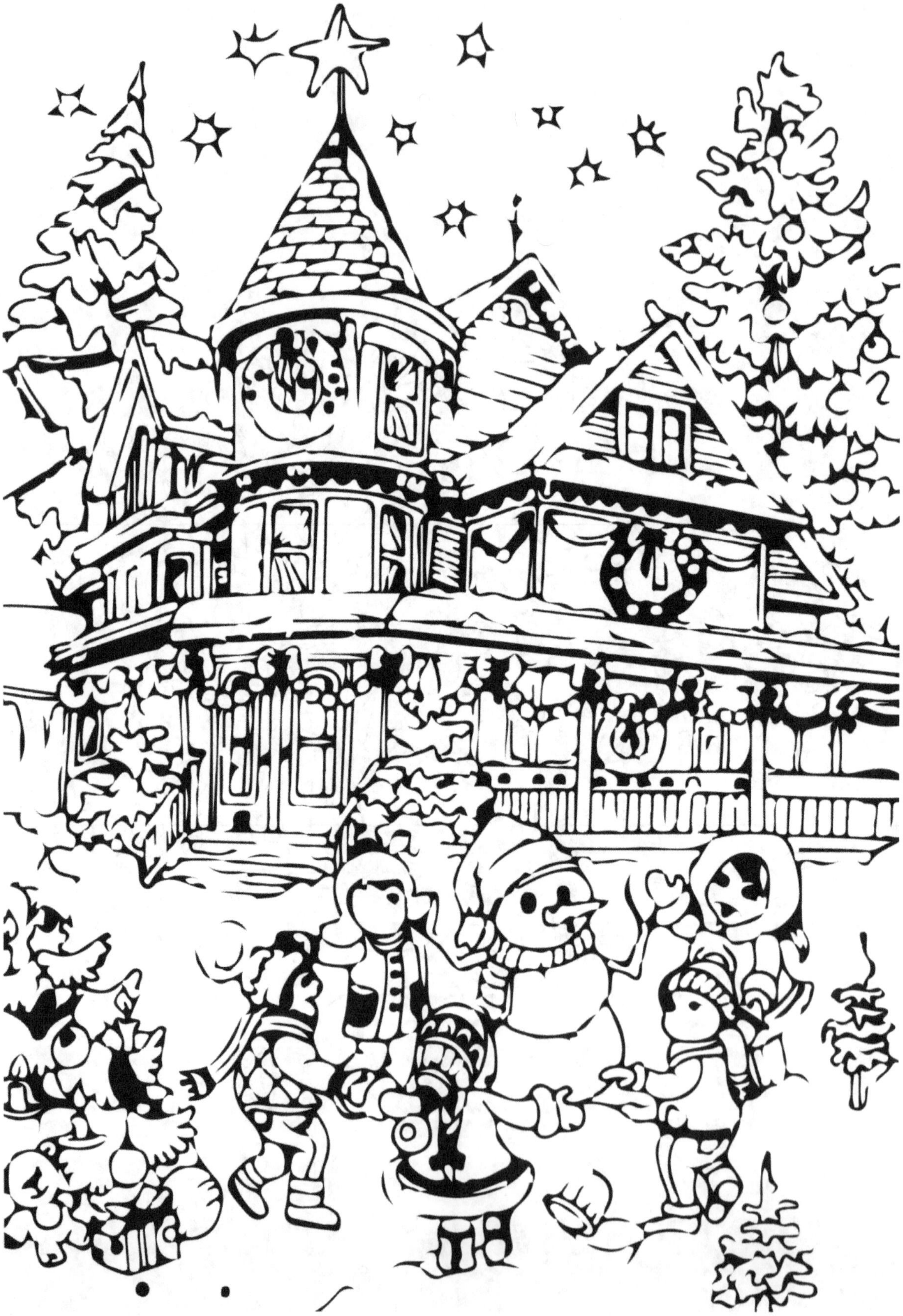

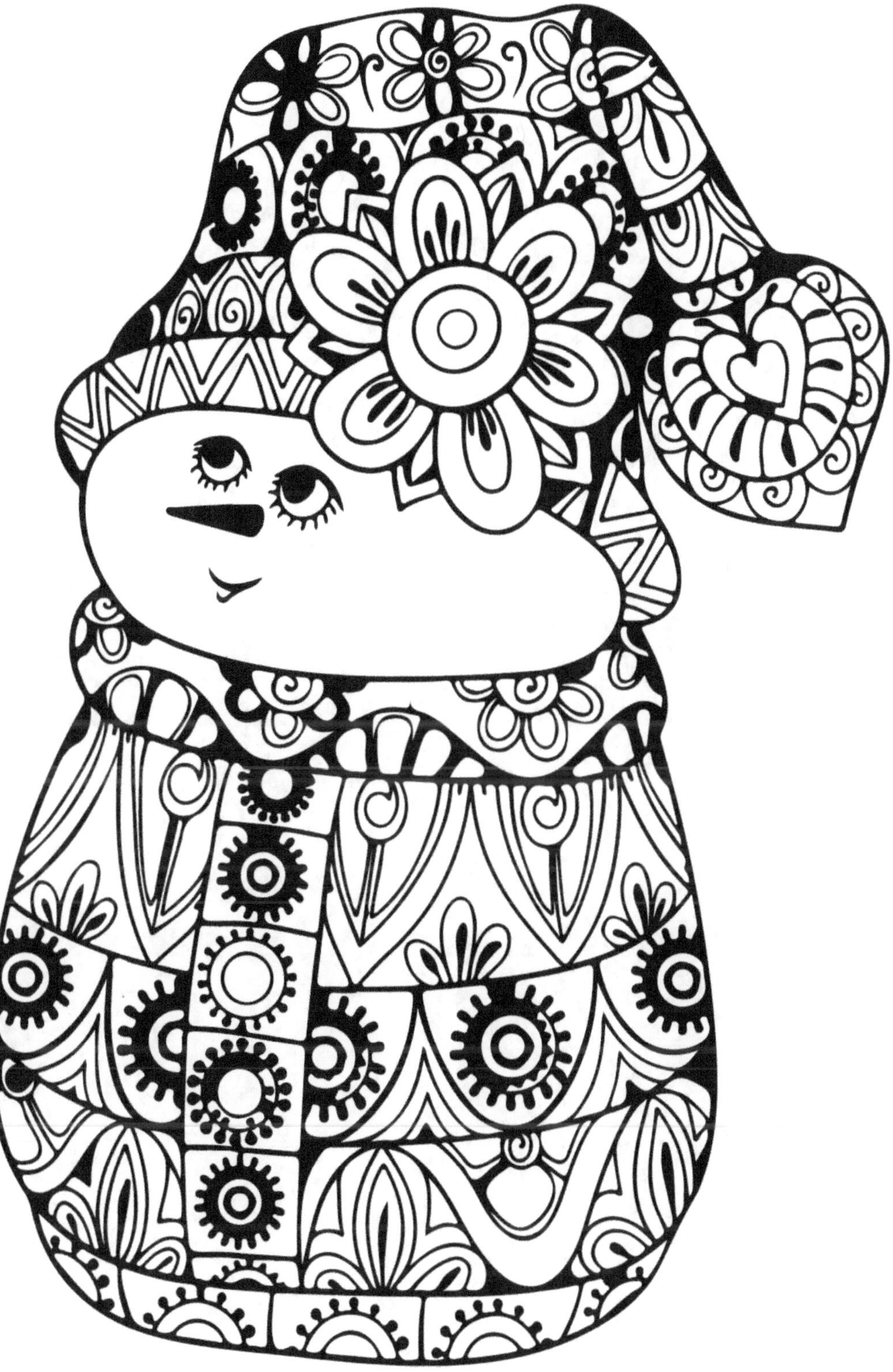

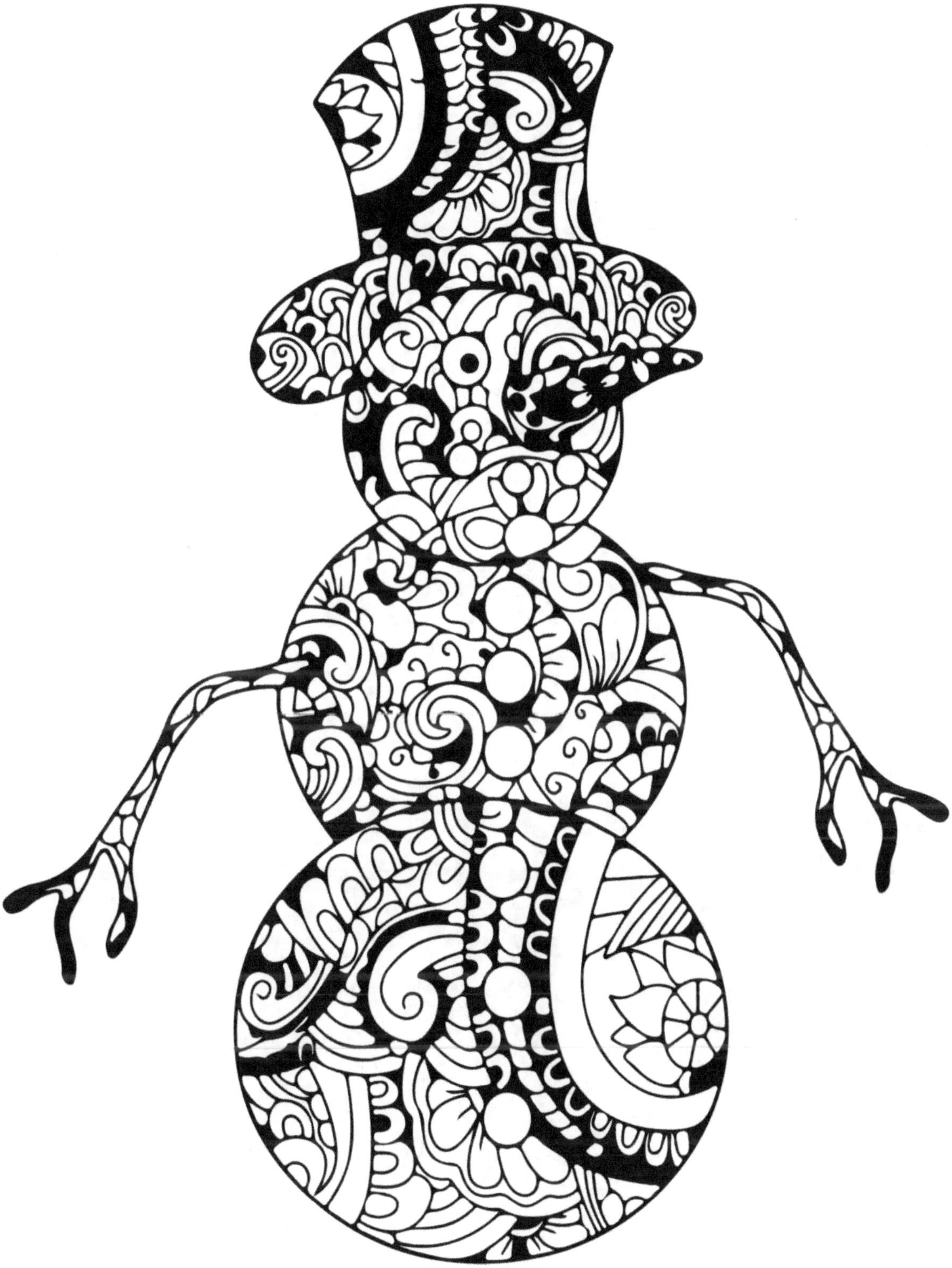

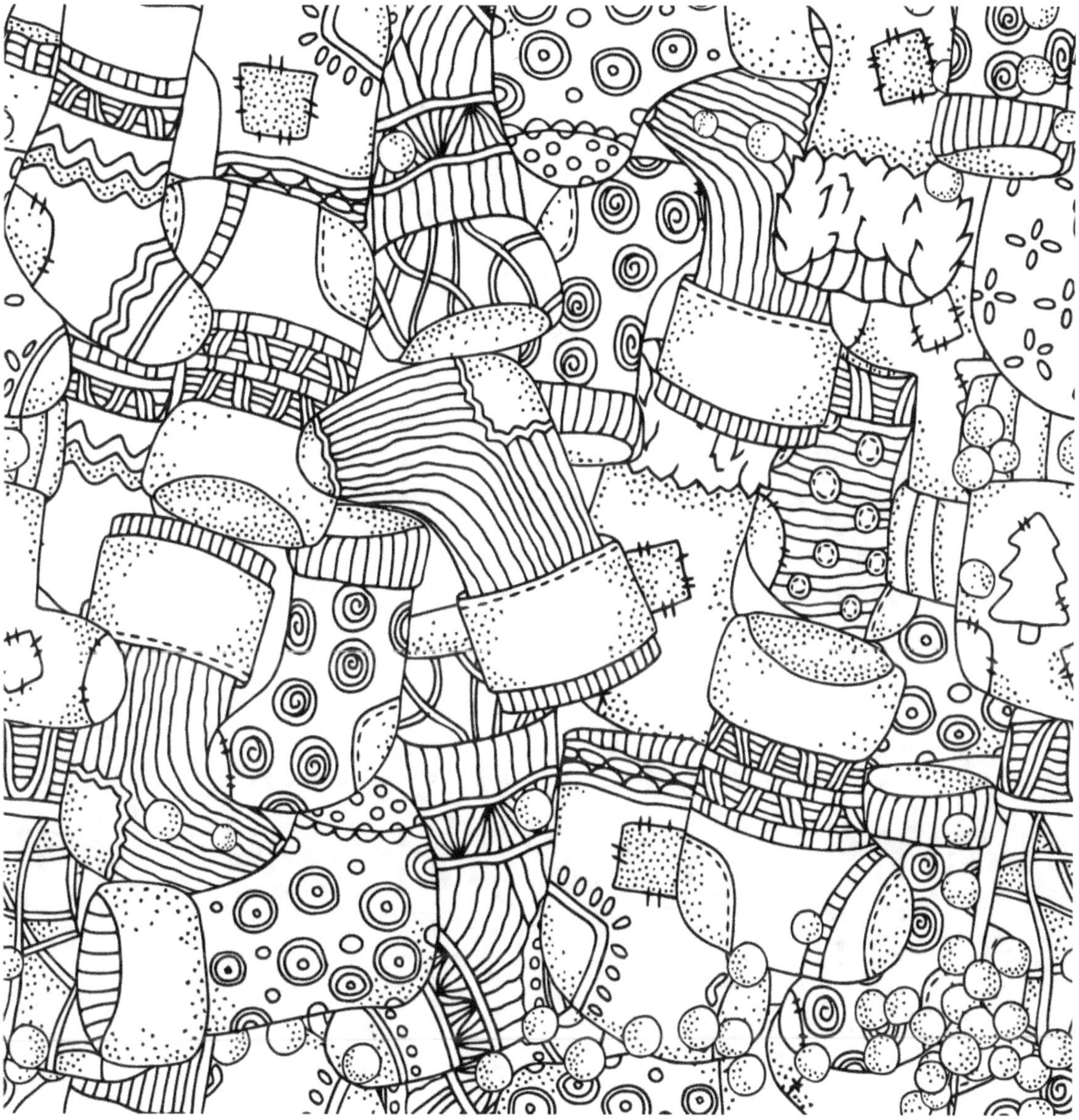

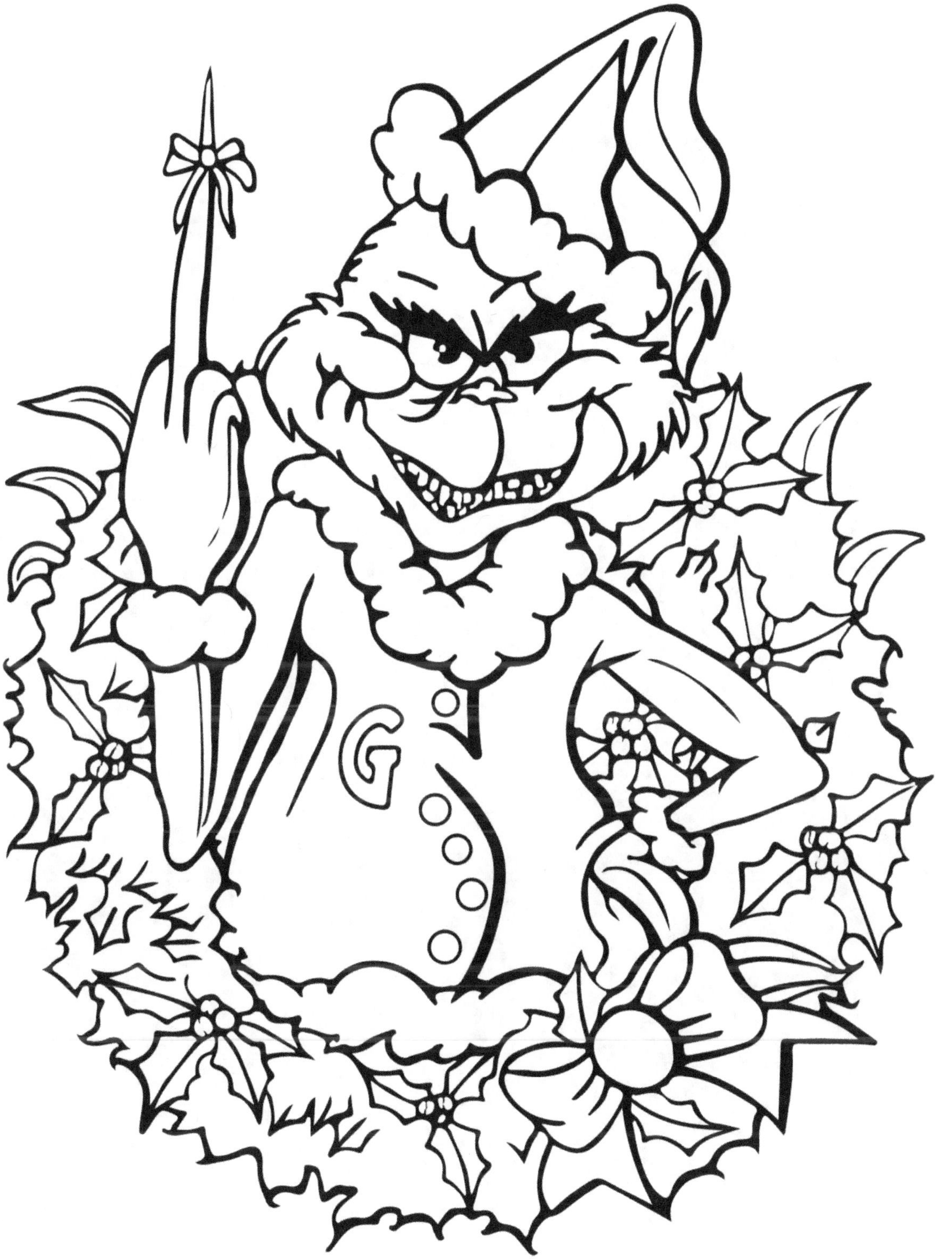
G

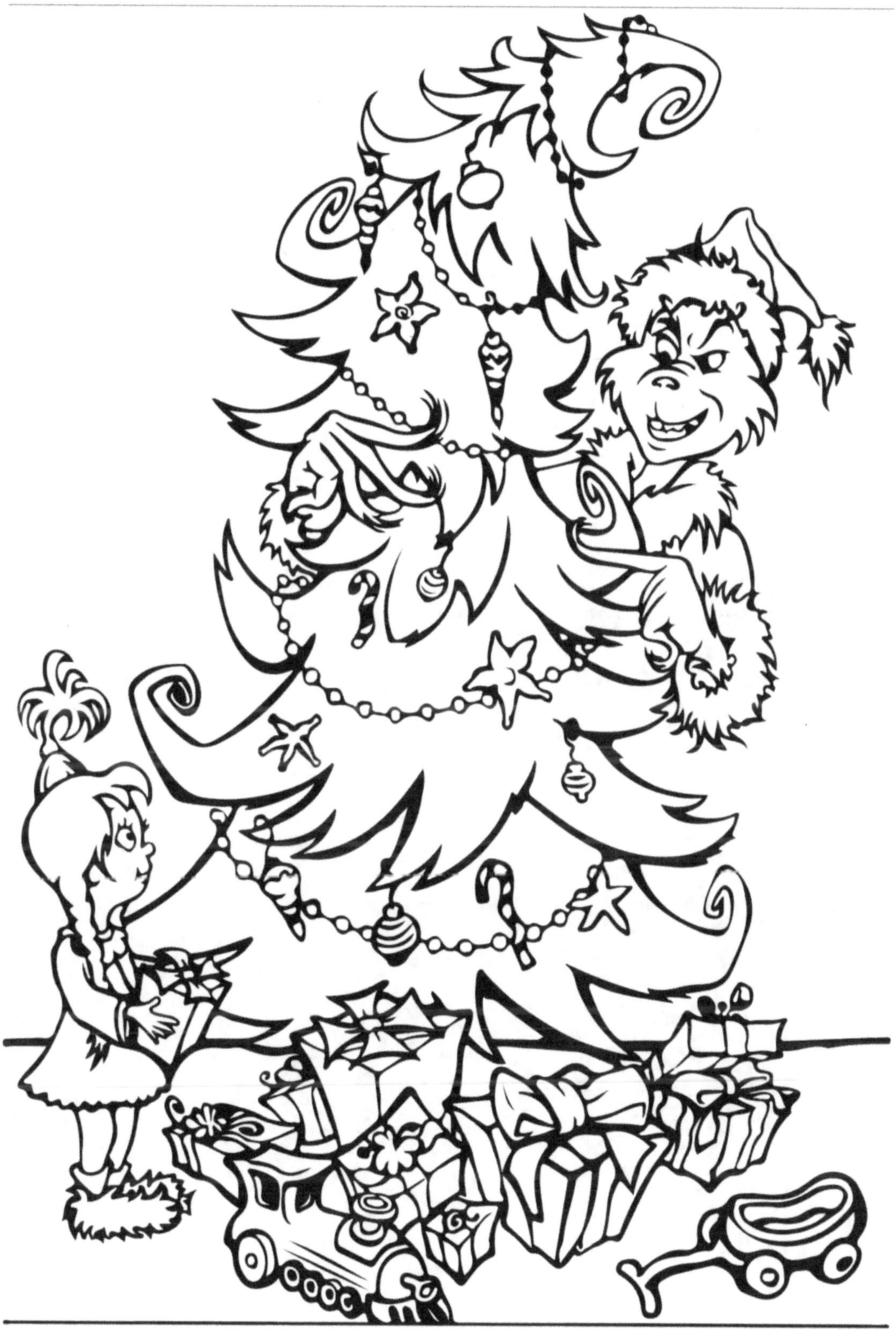

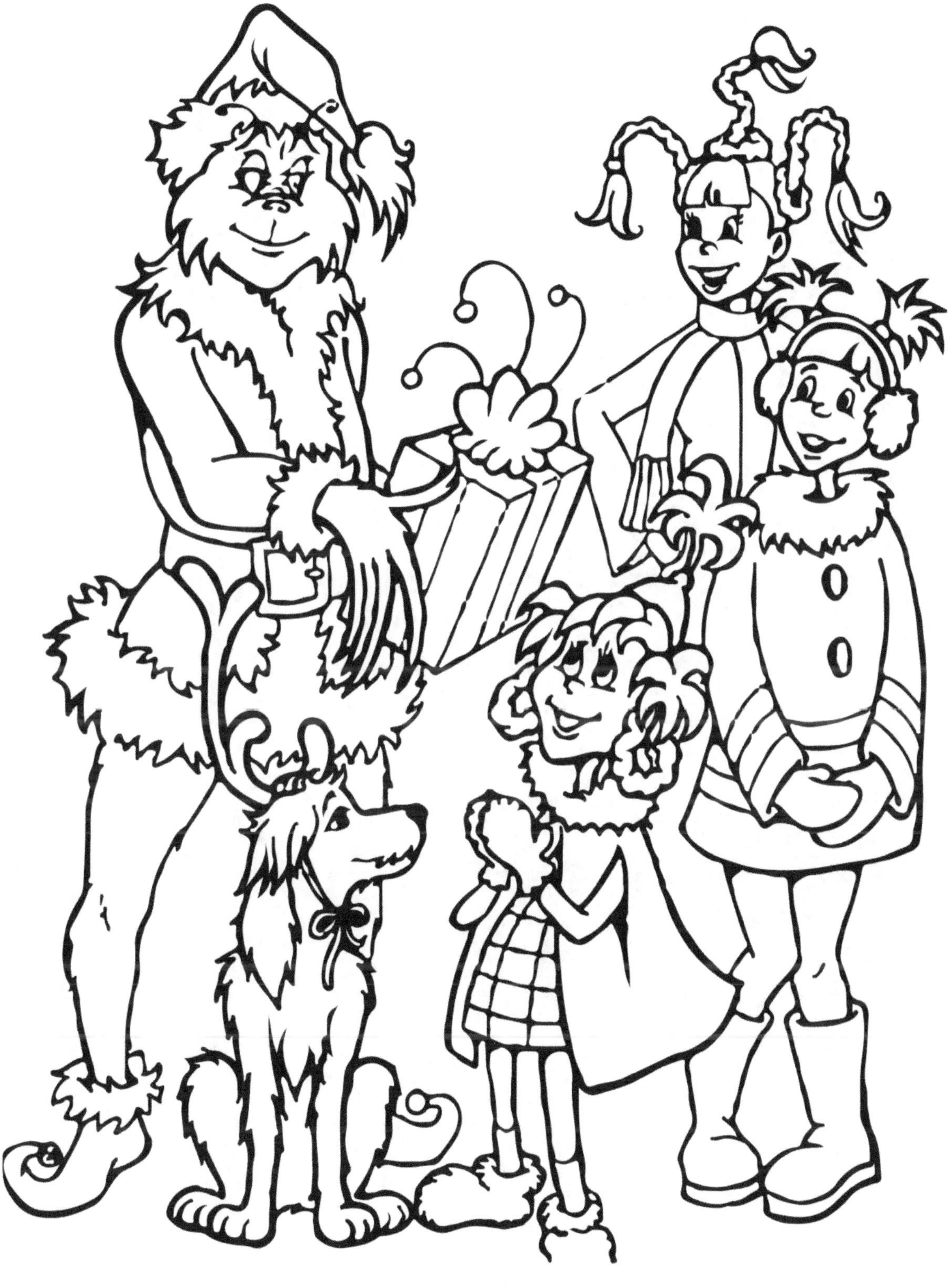

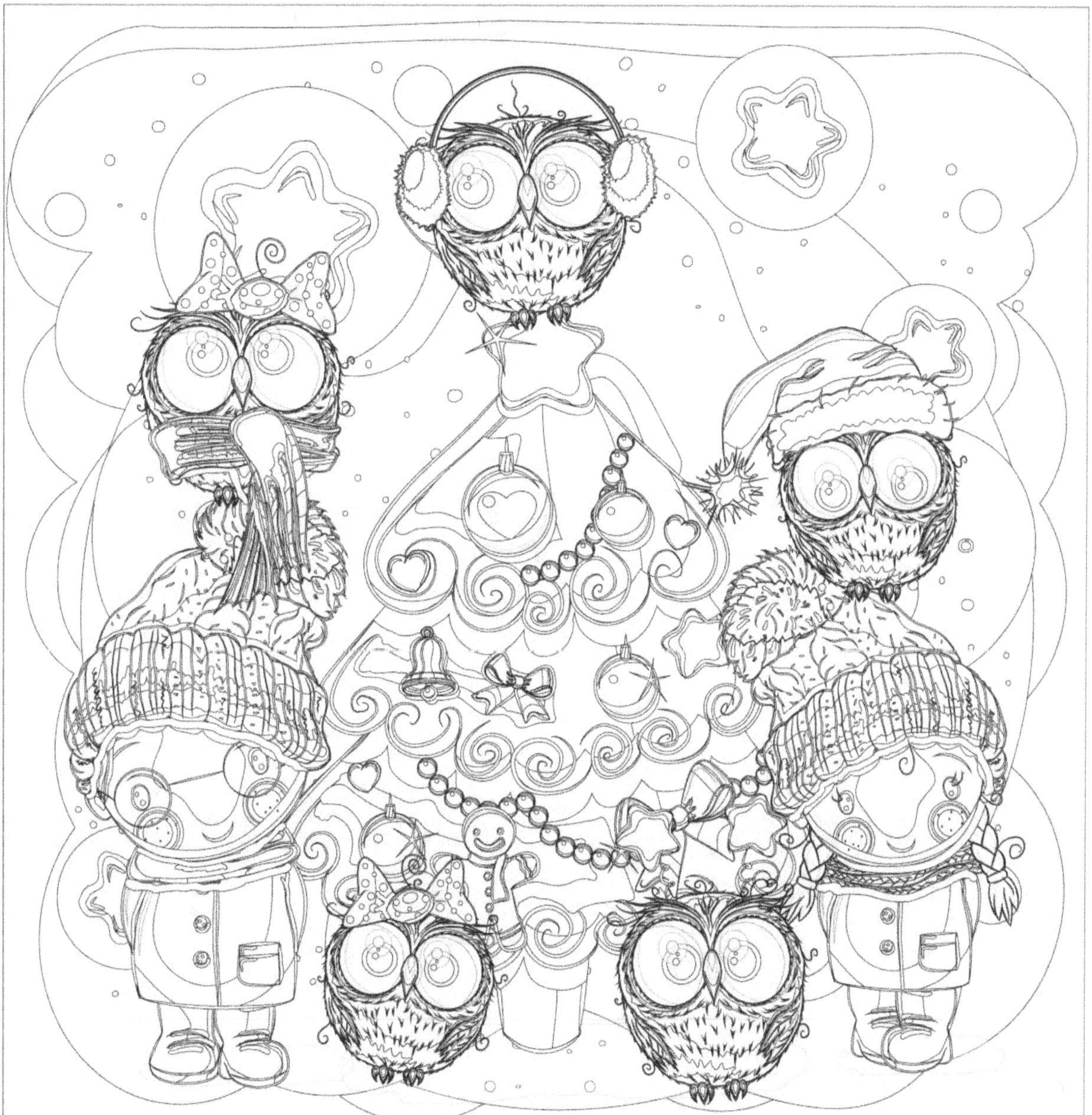

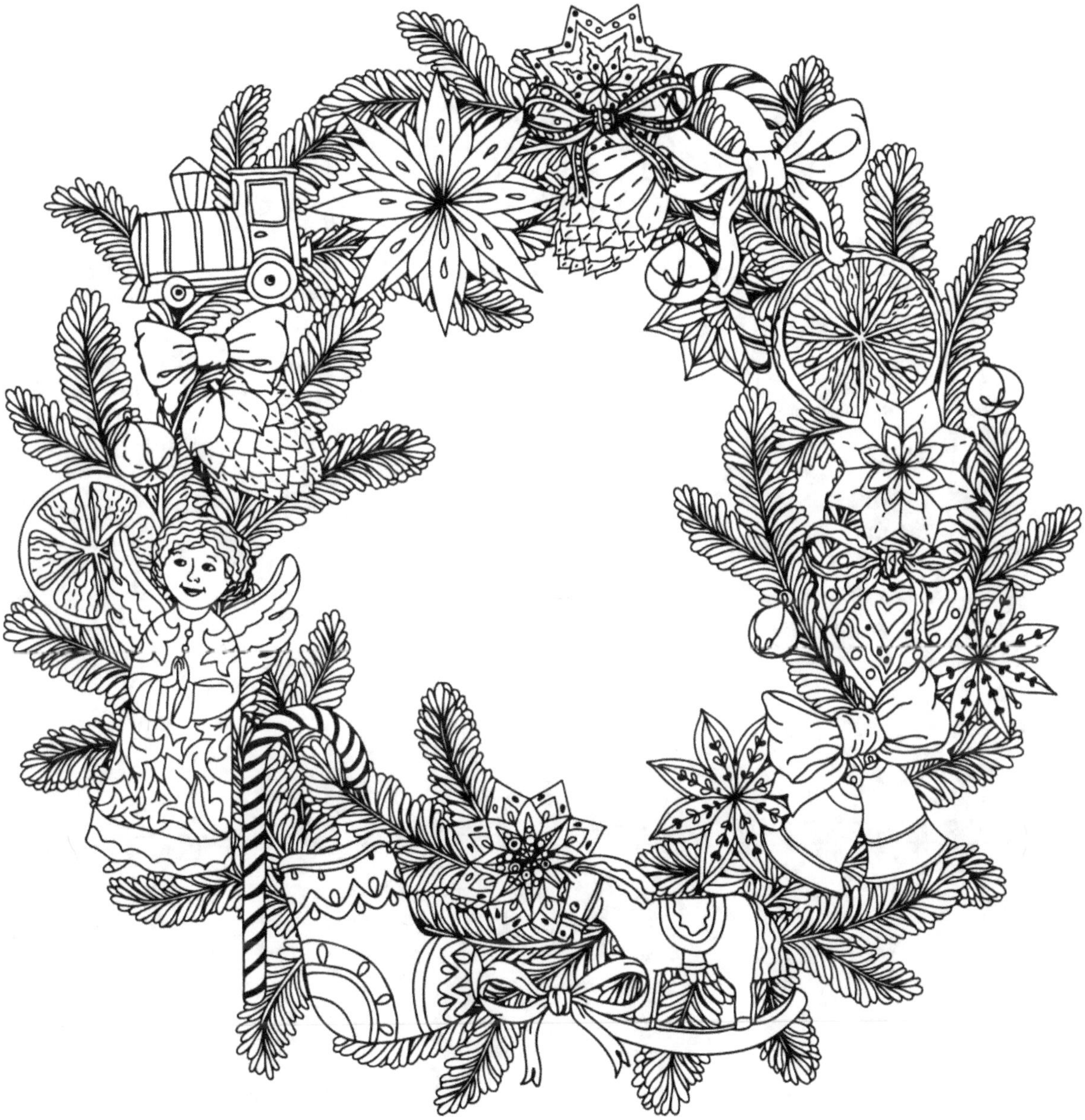

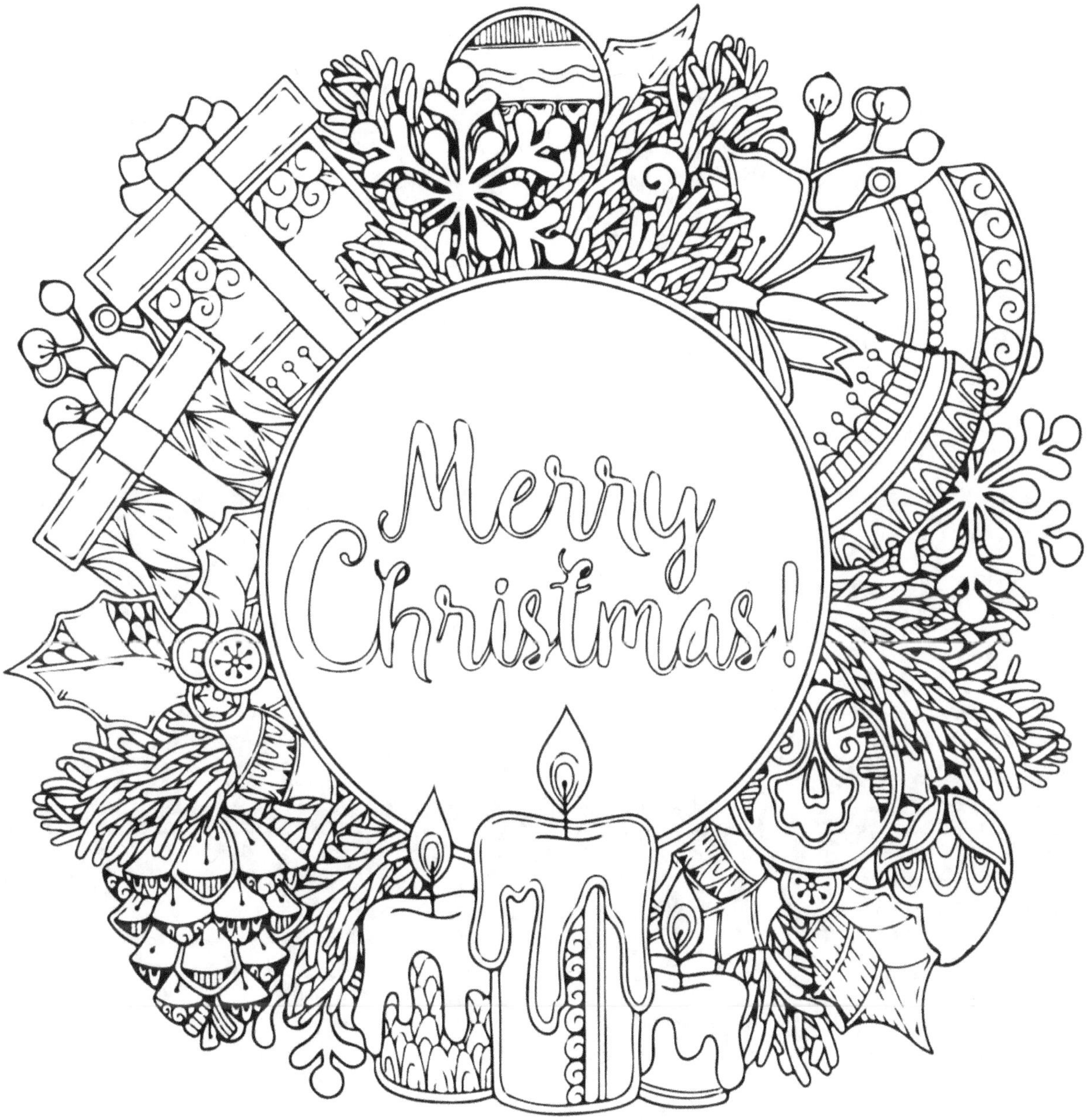
Merry Christmas!

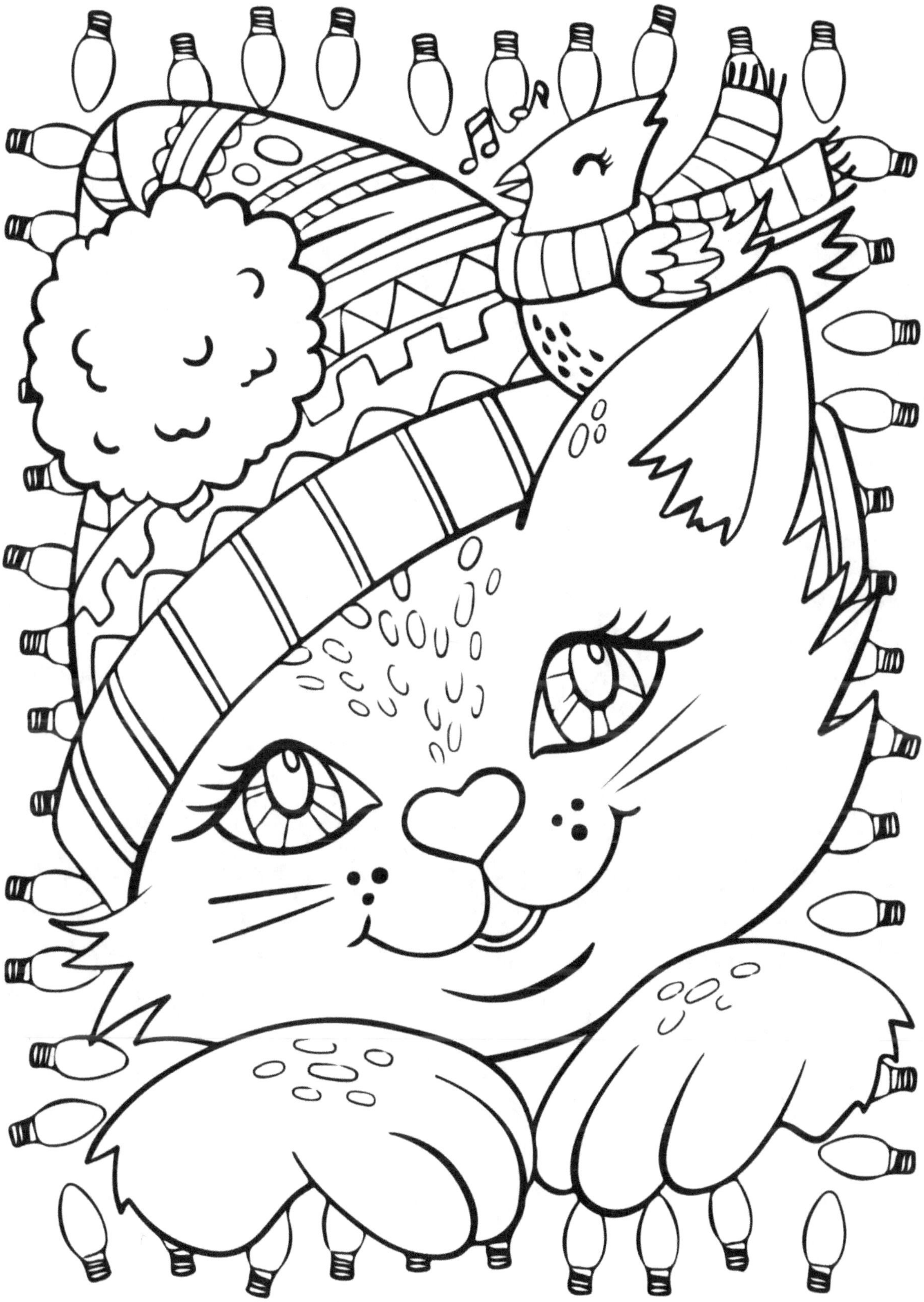

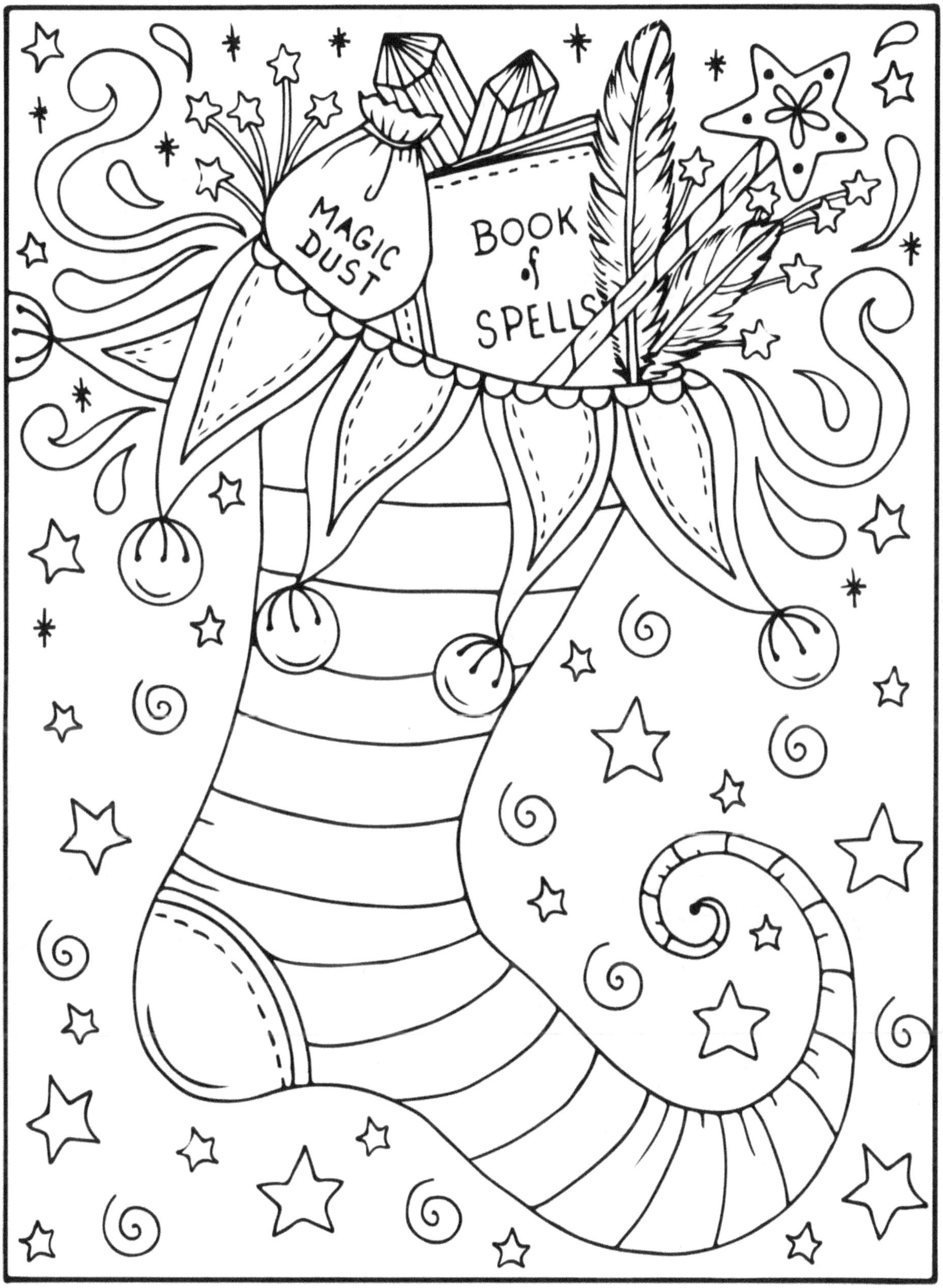
MAGIC DUST
BOOK of SPELLS

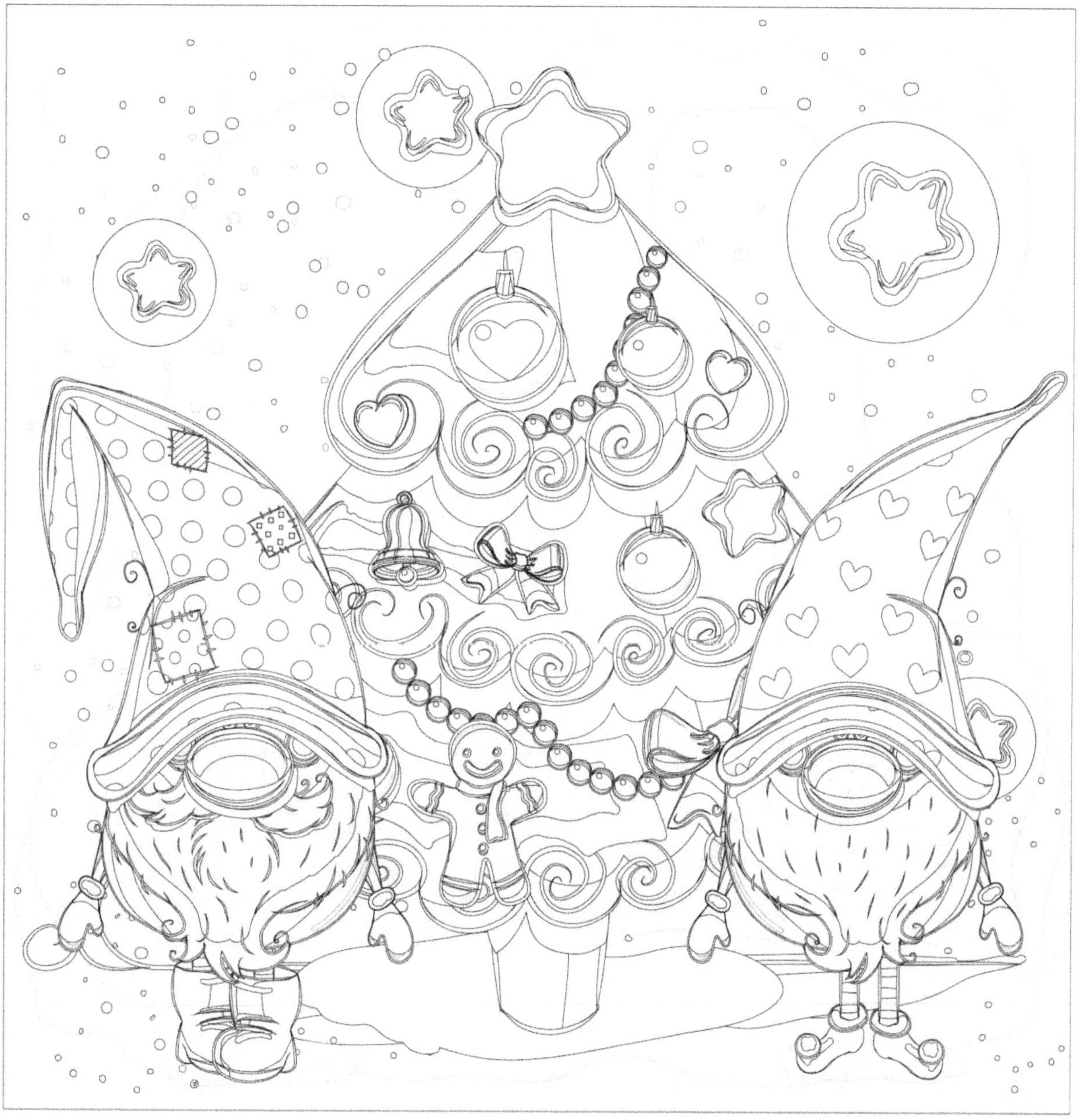

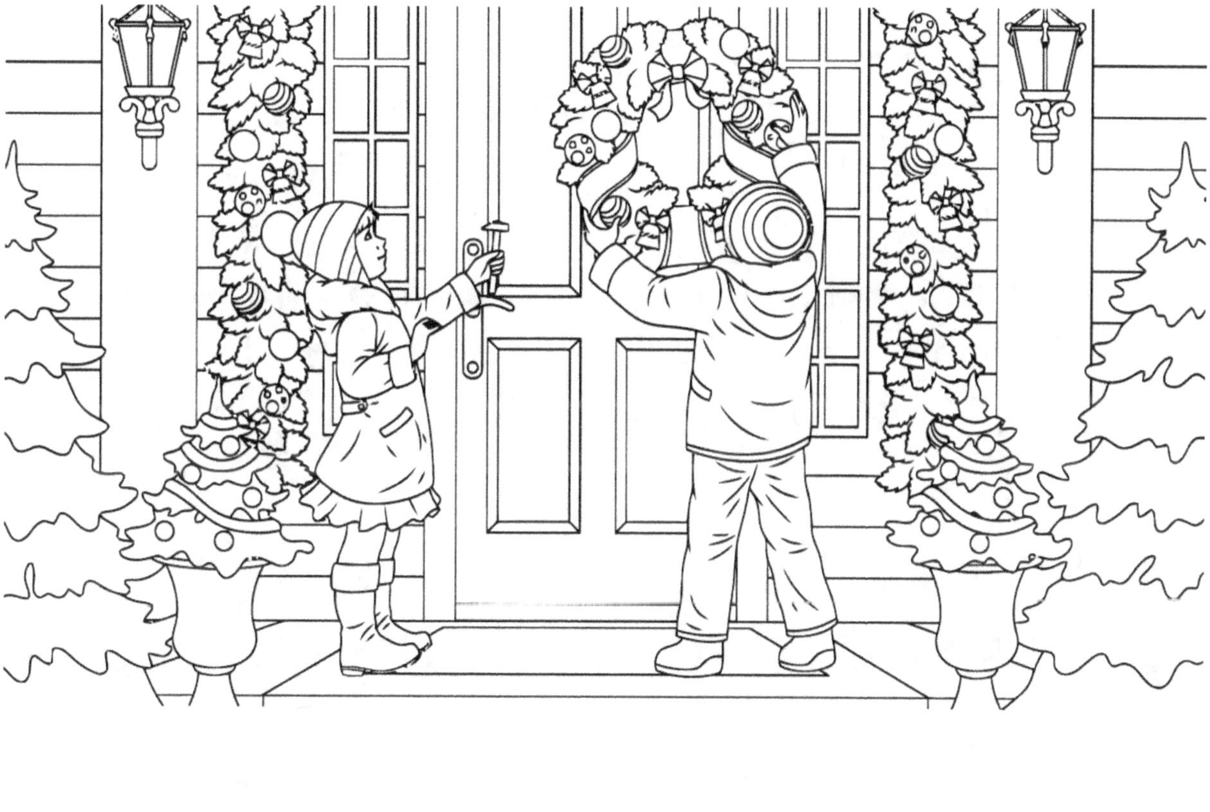

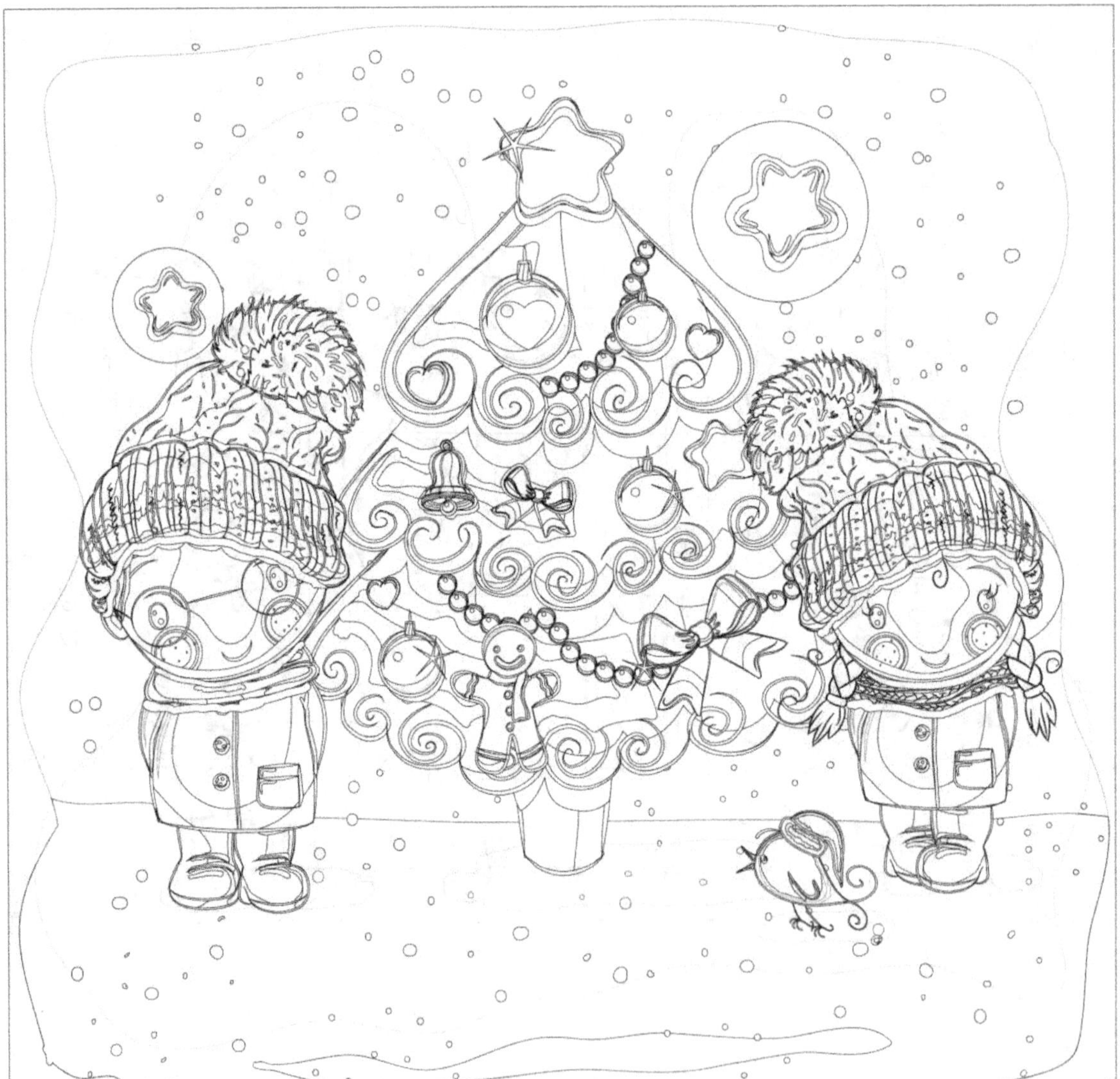

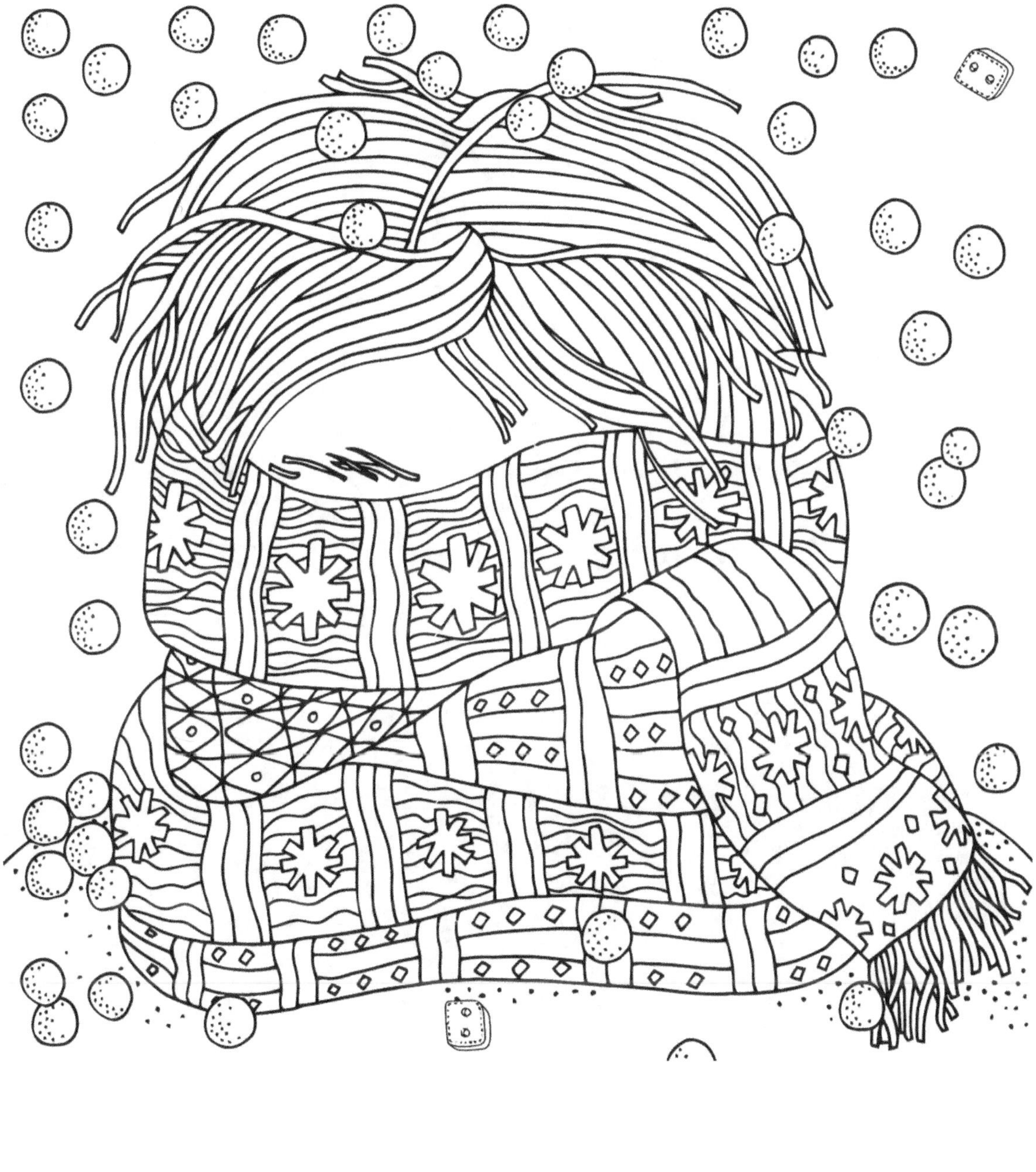

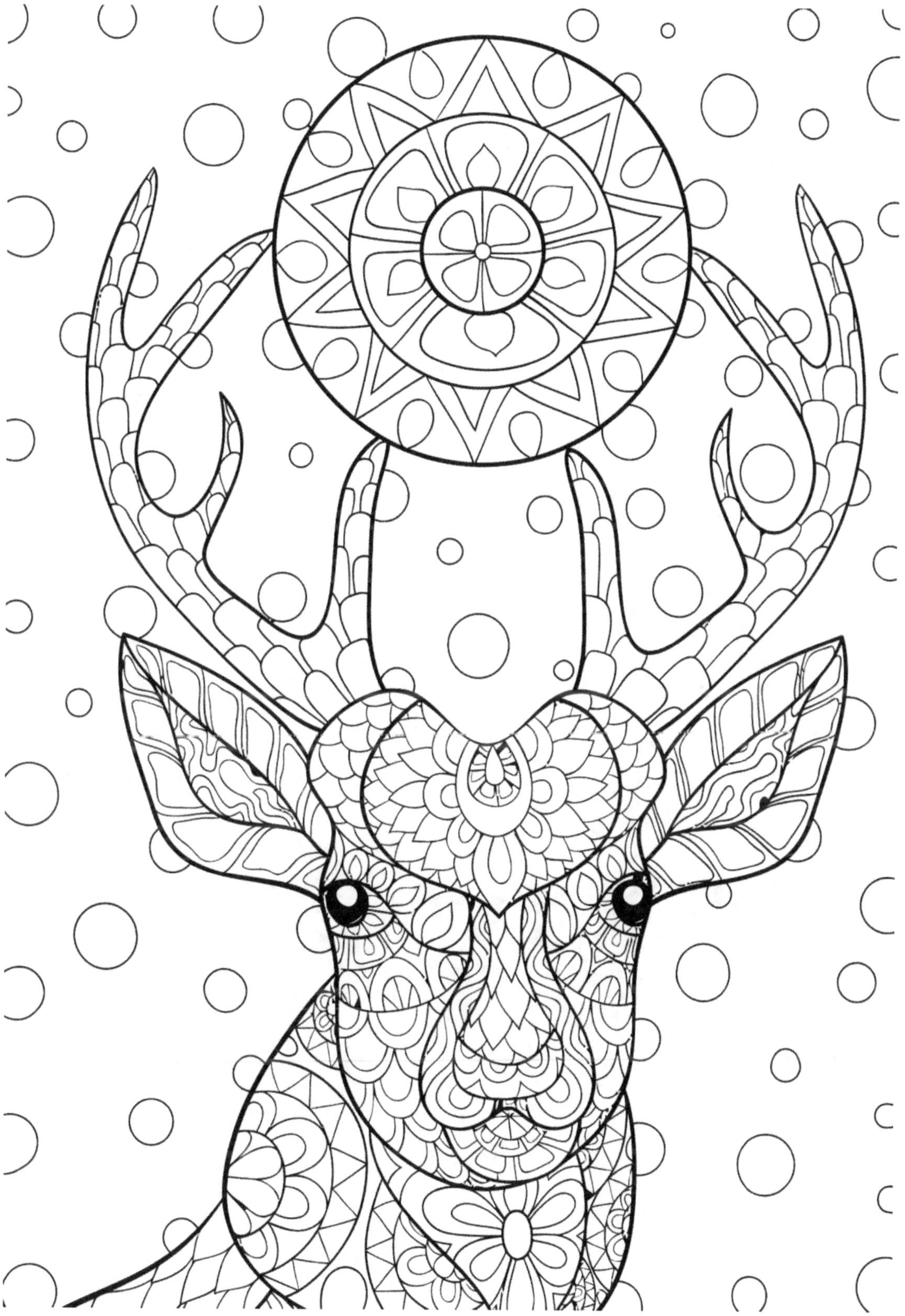

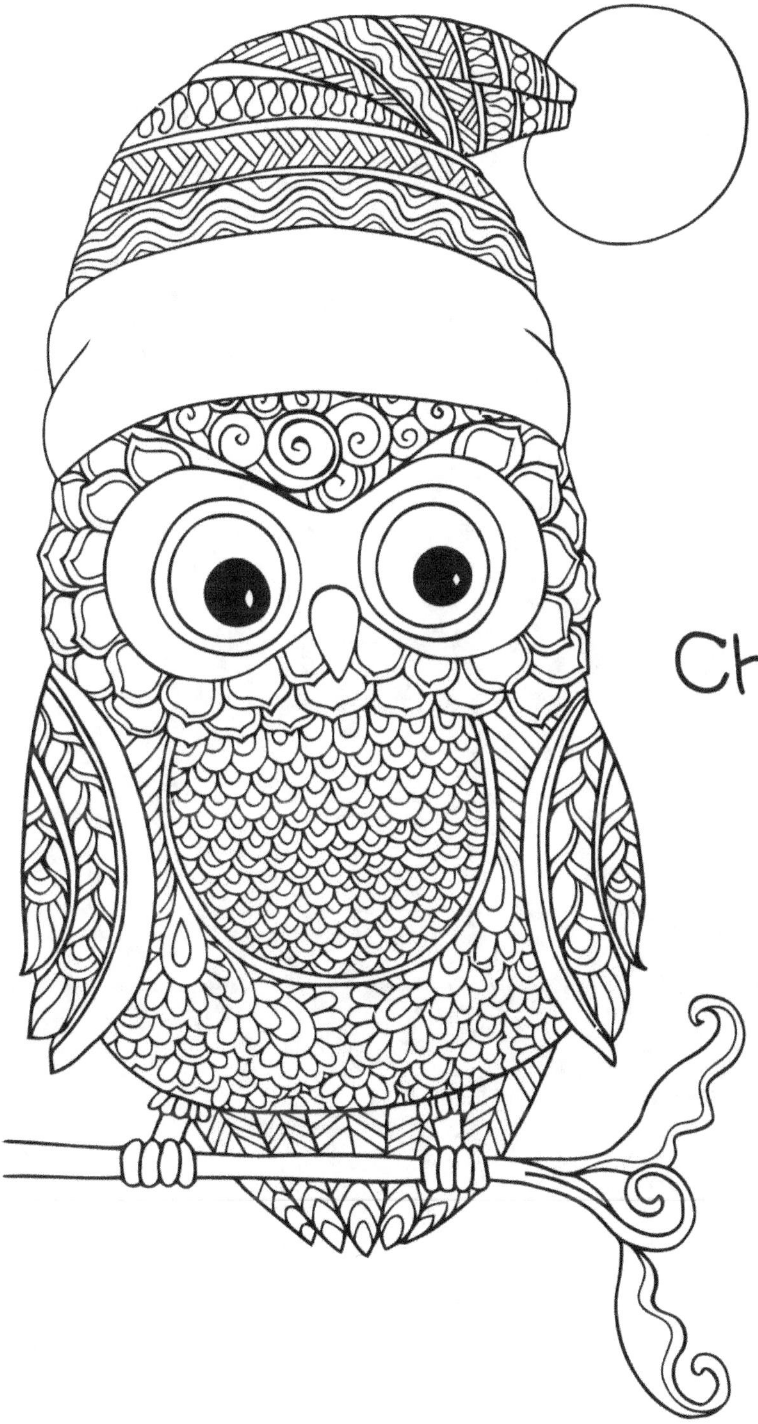

Merry Christmas !

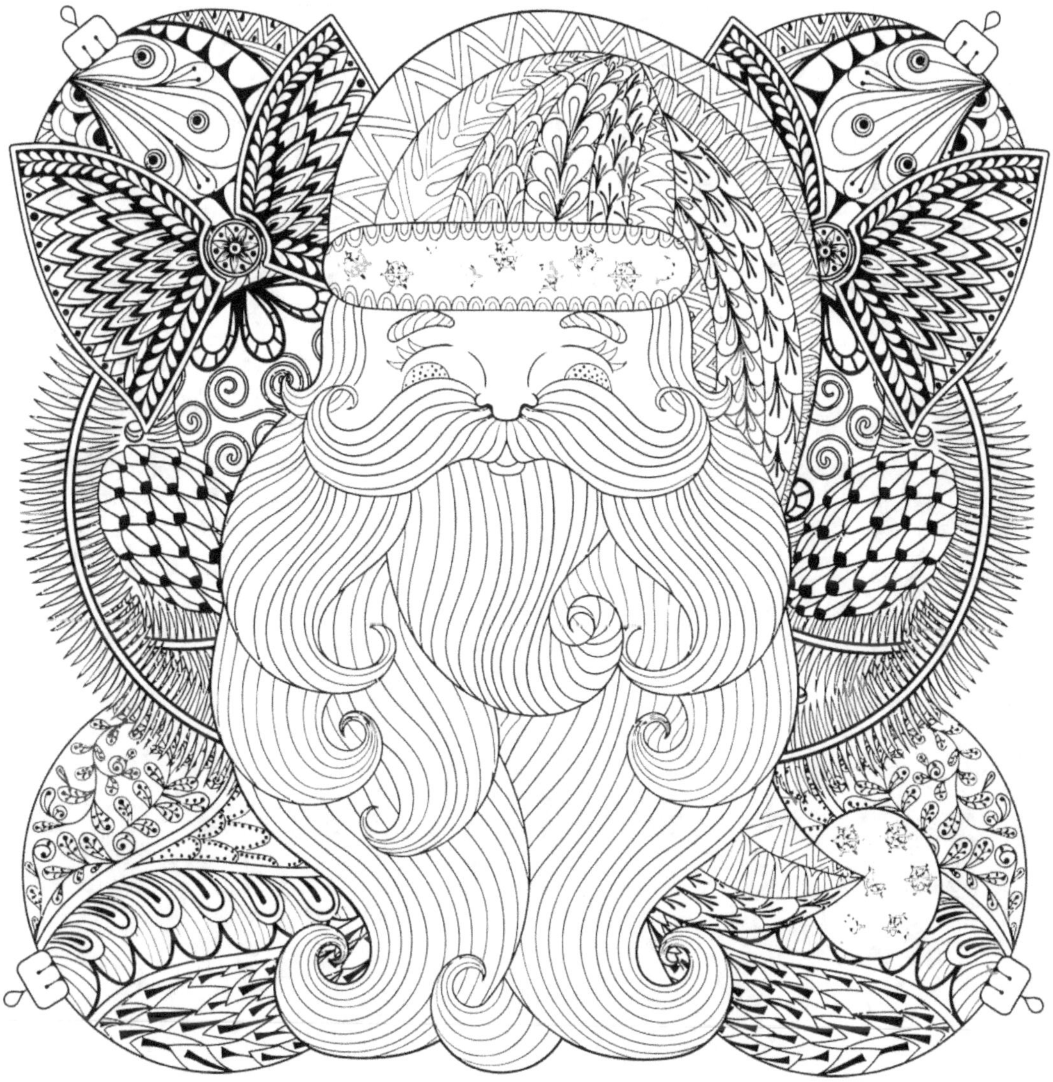

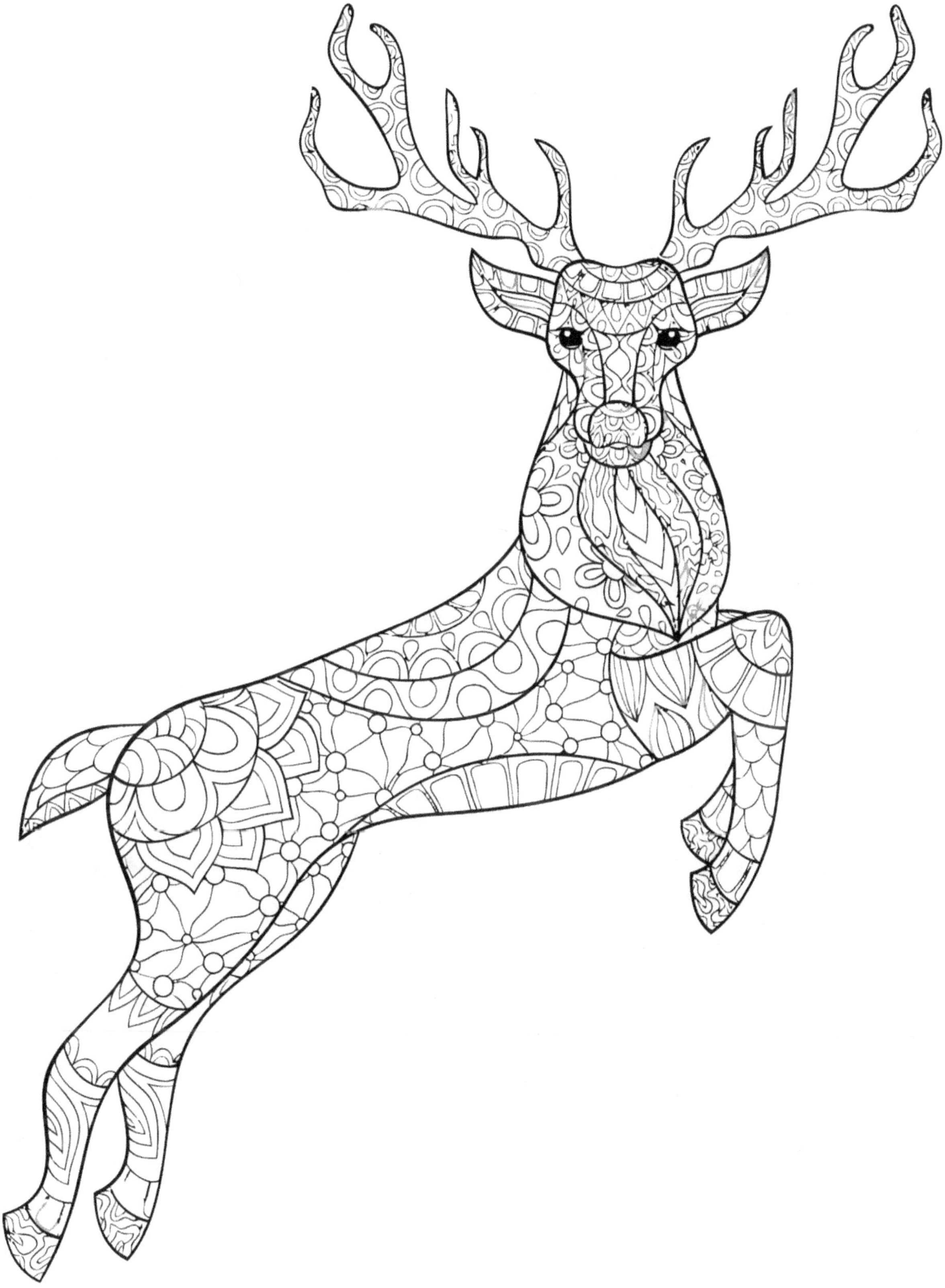

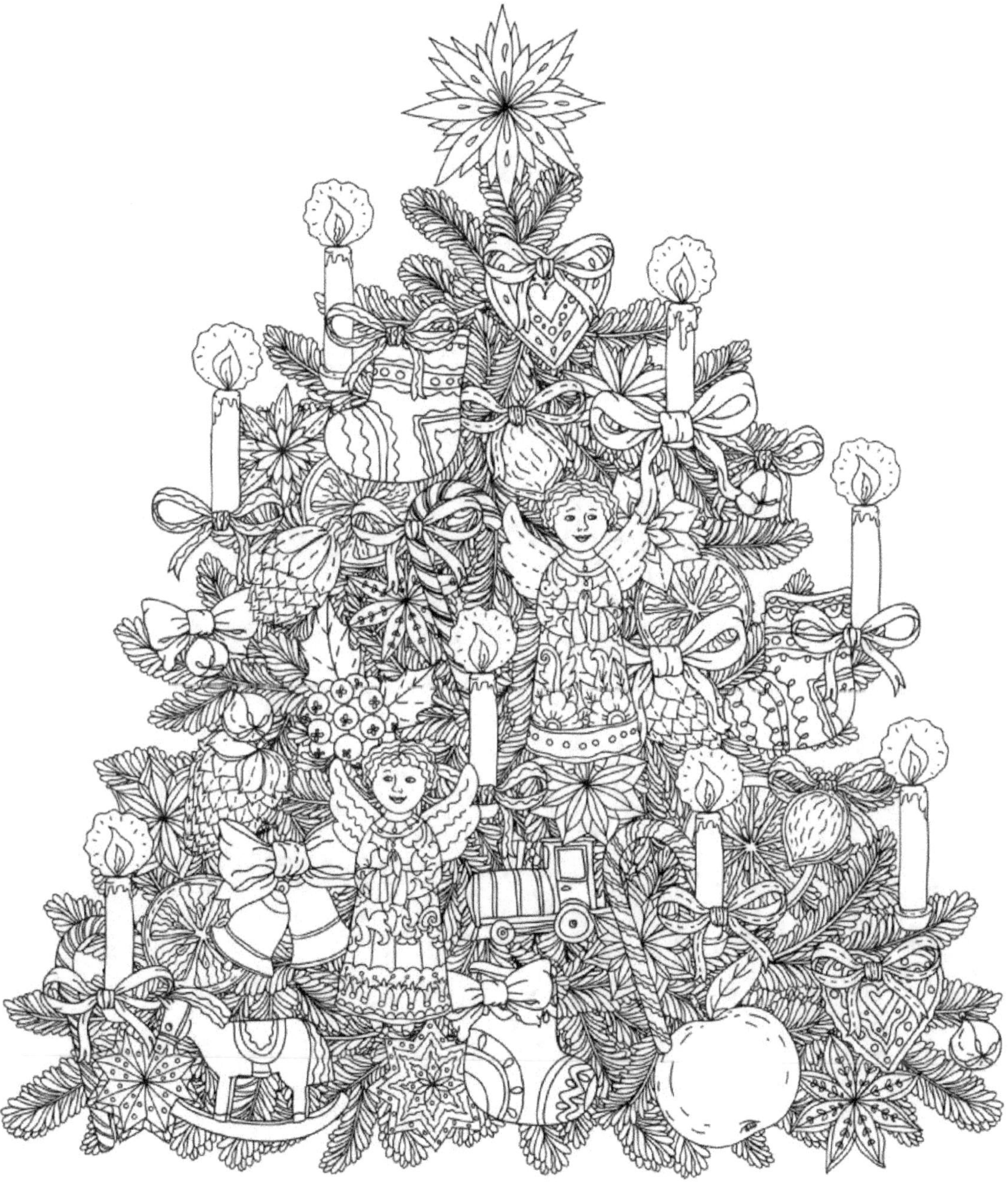

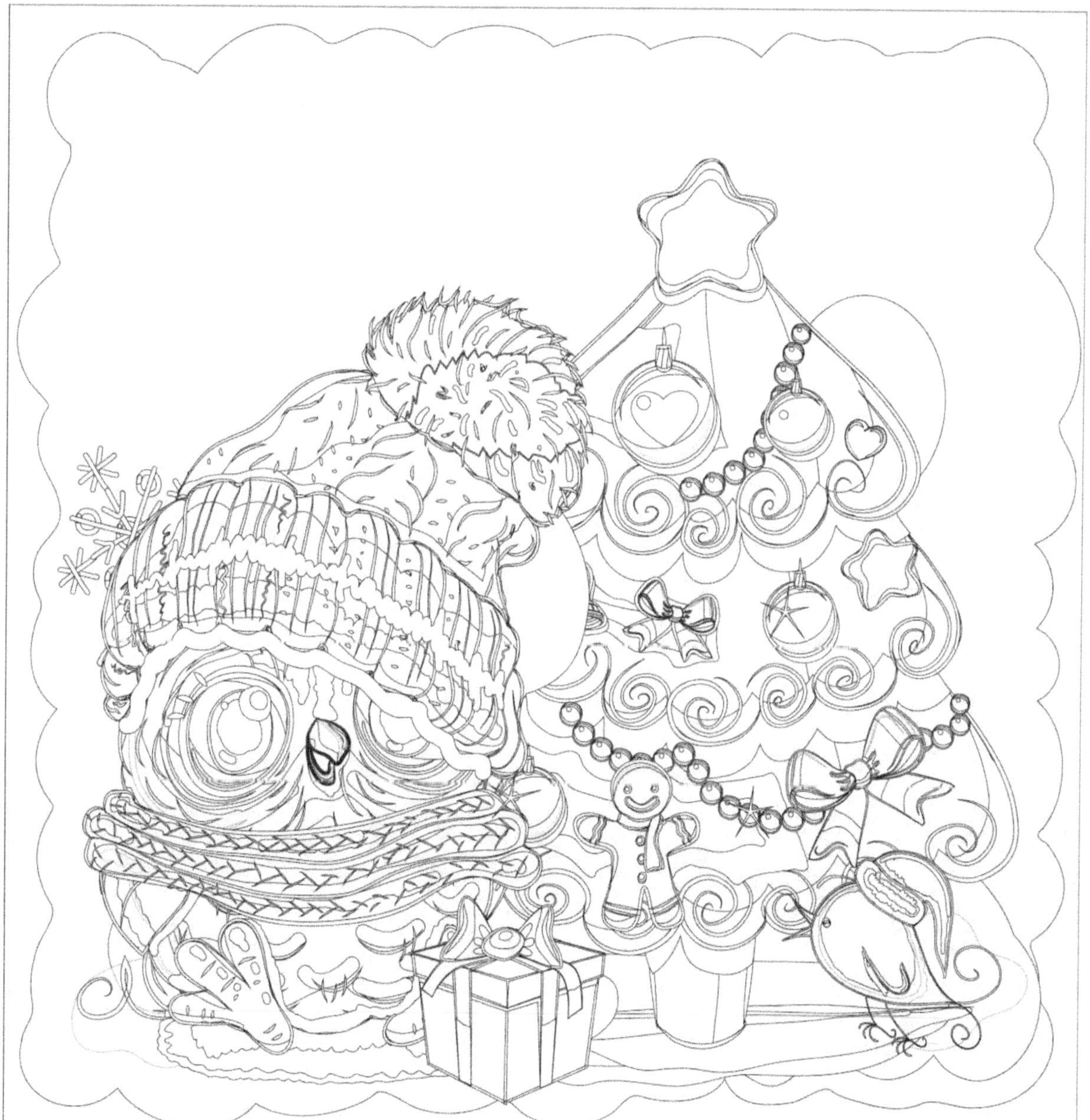

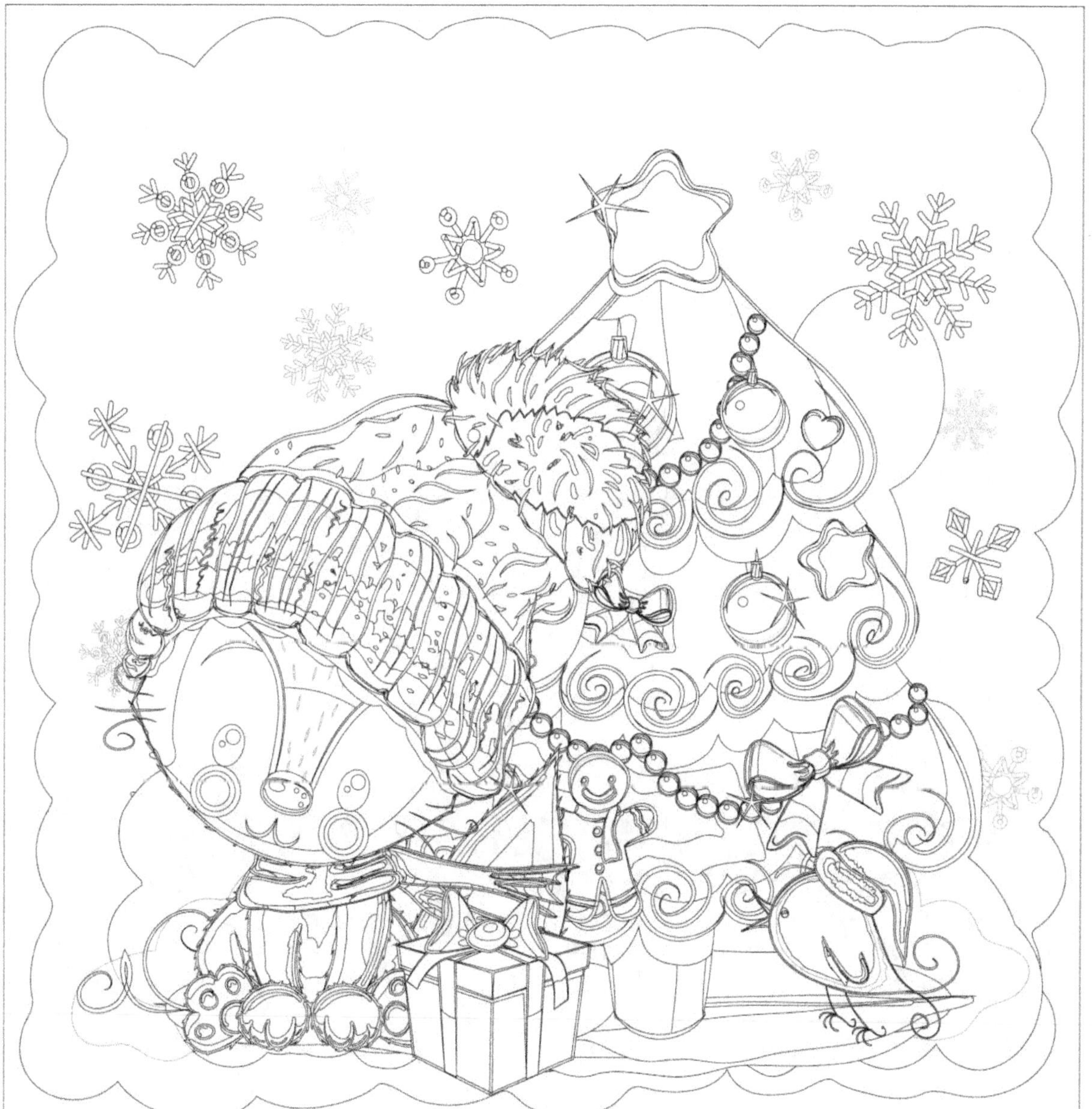

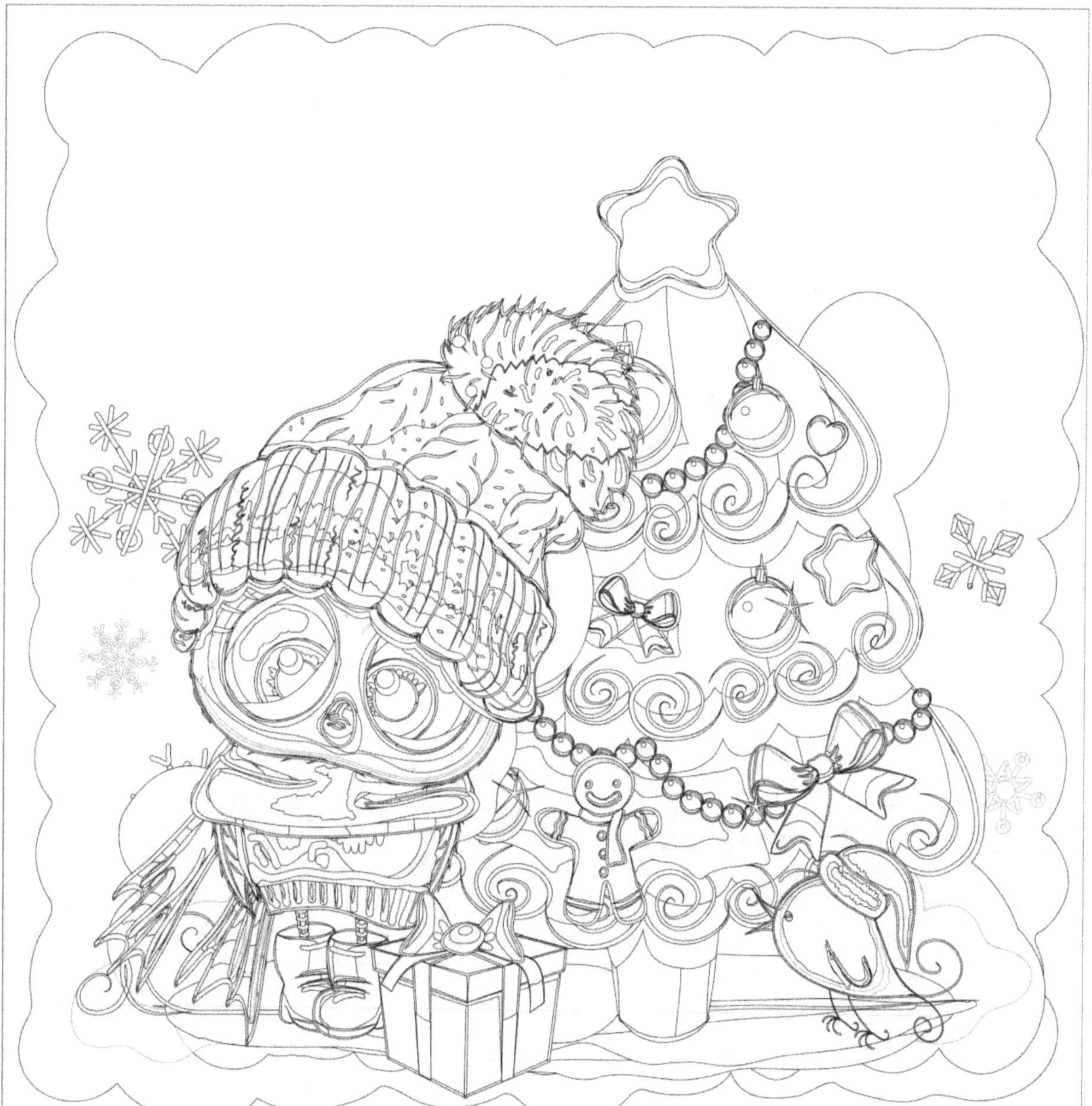

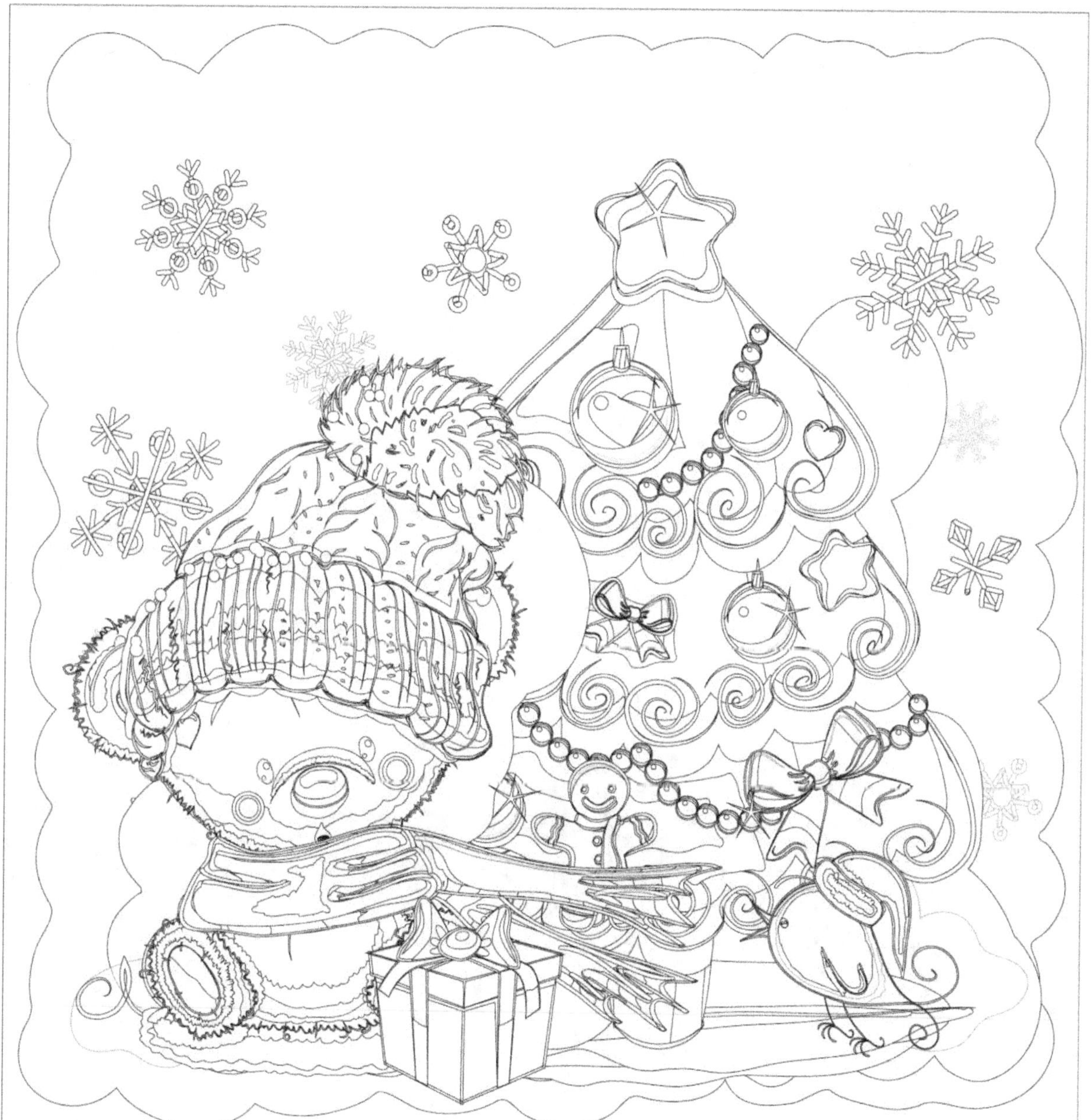

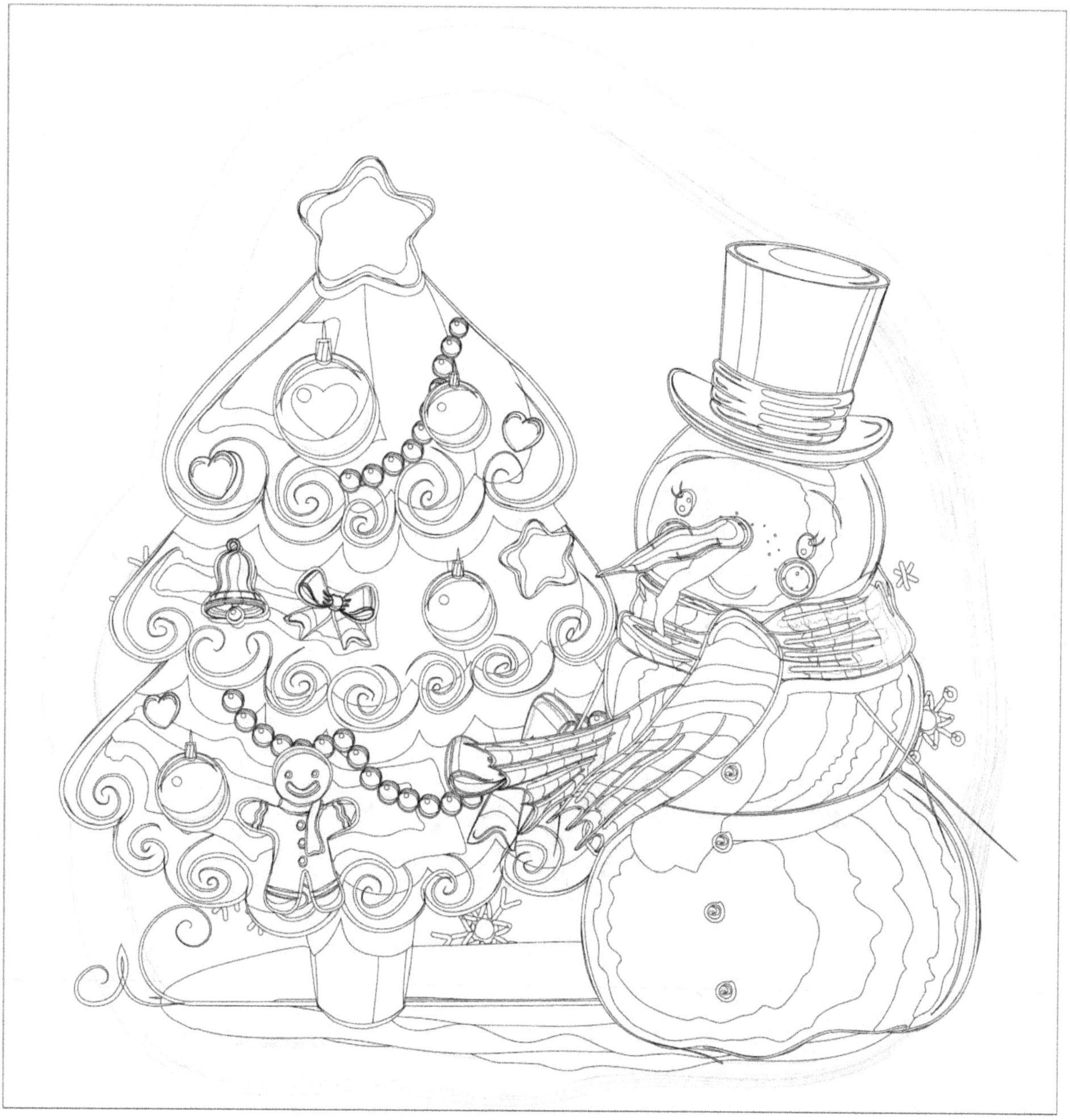

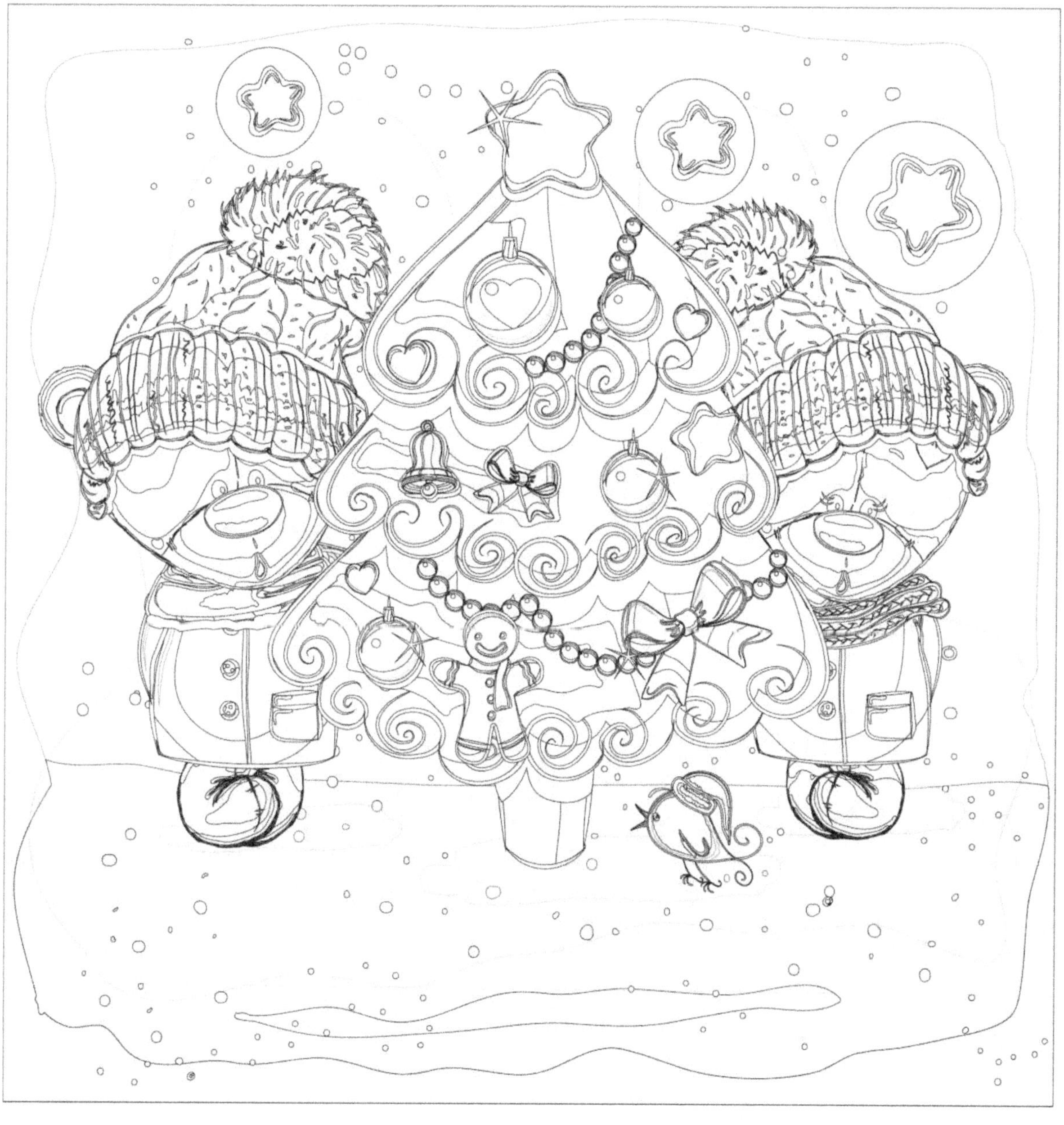

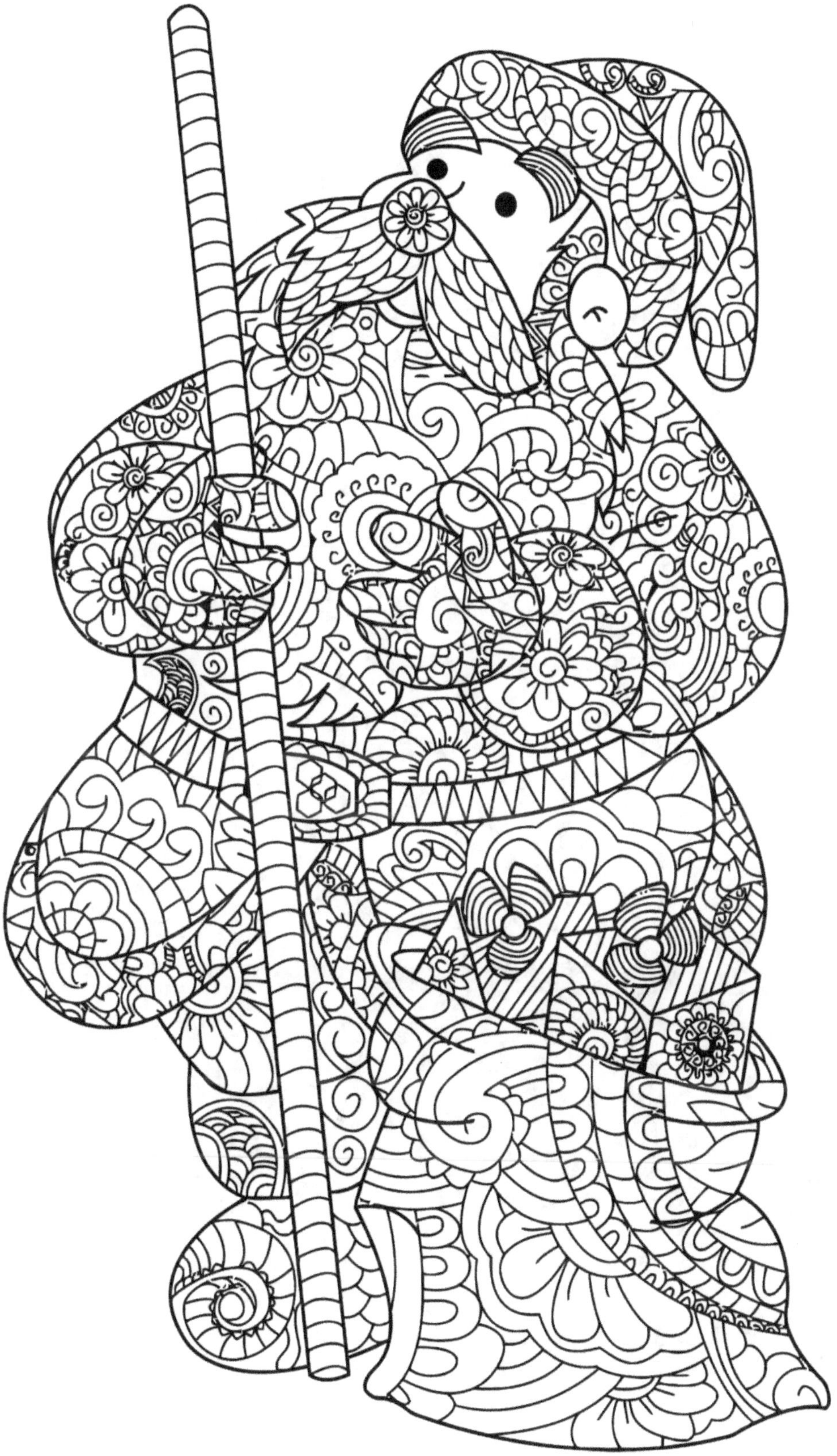

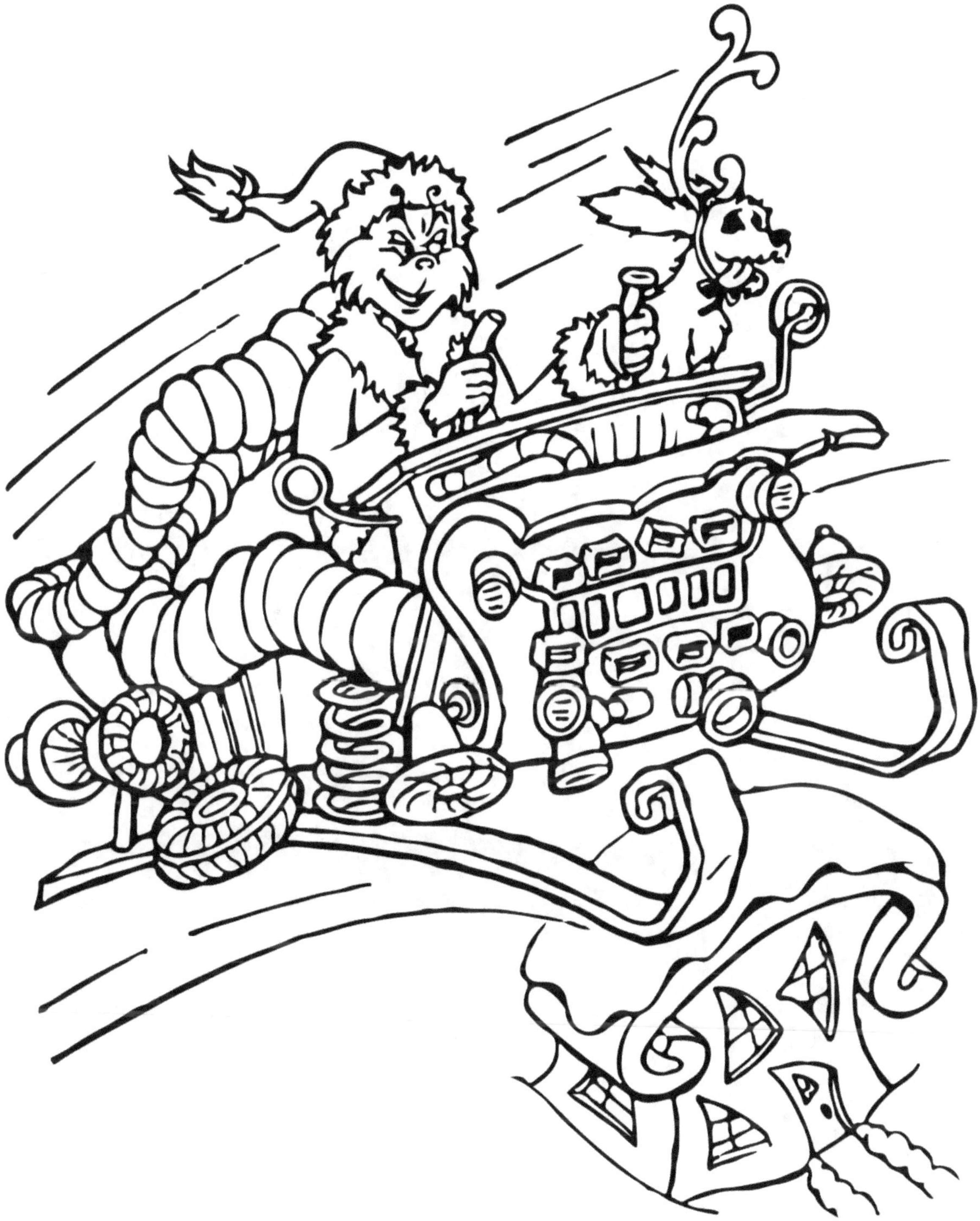

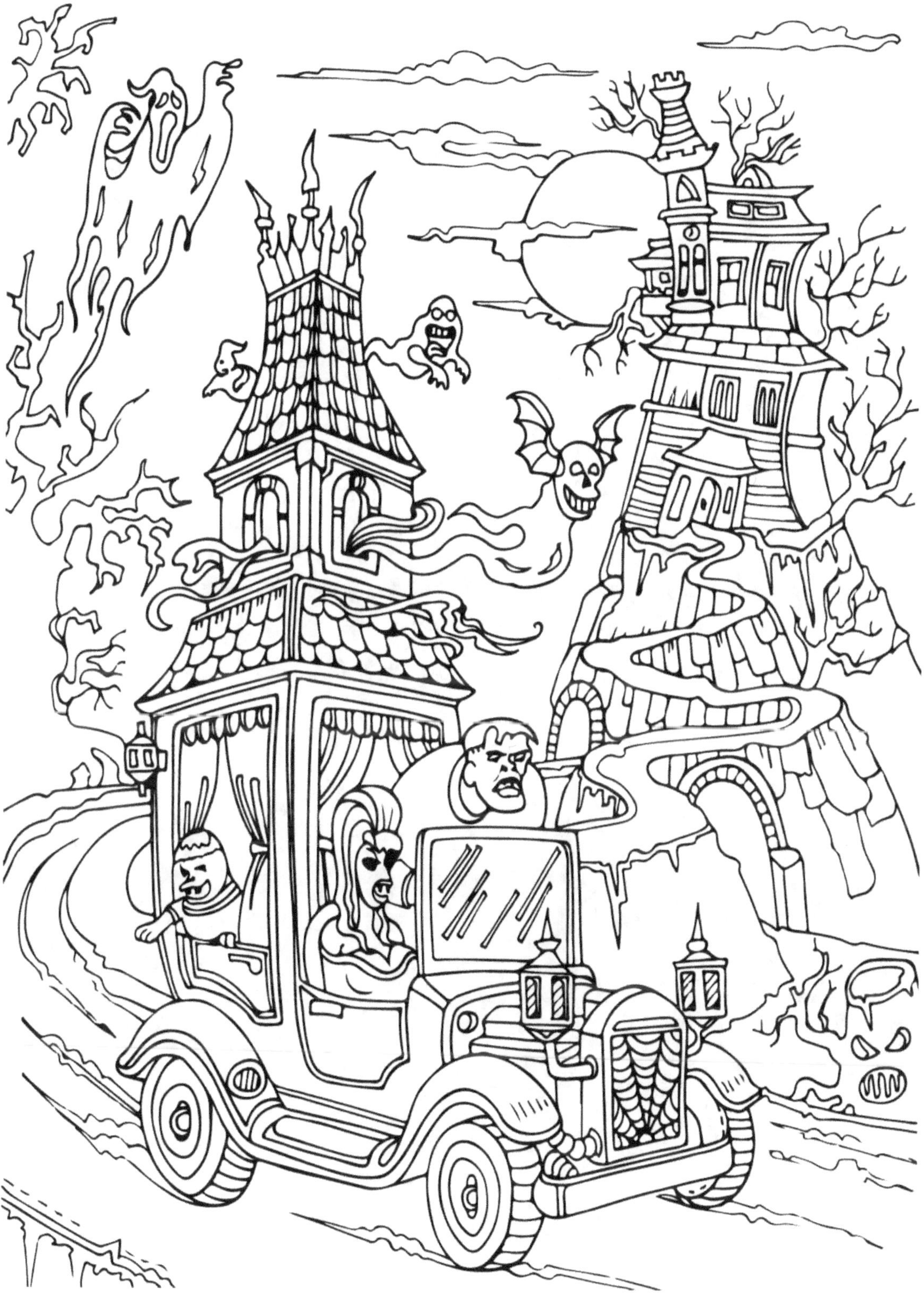

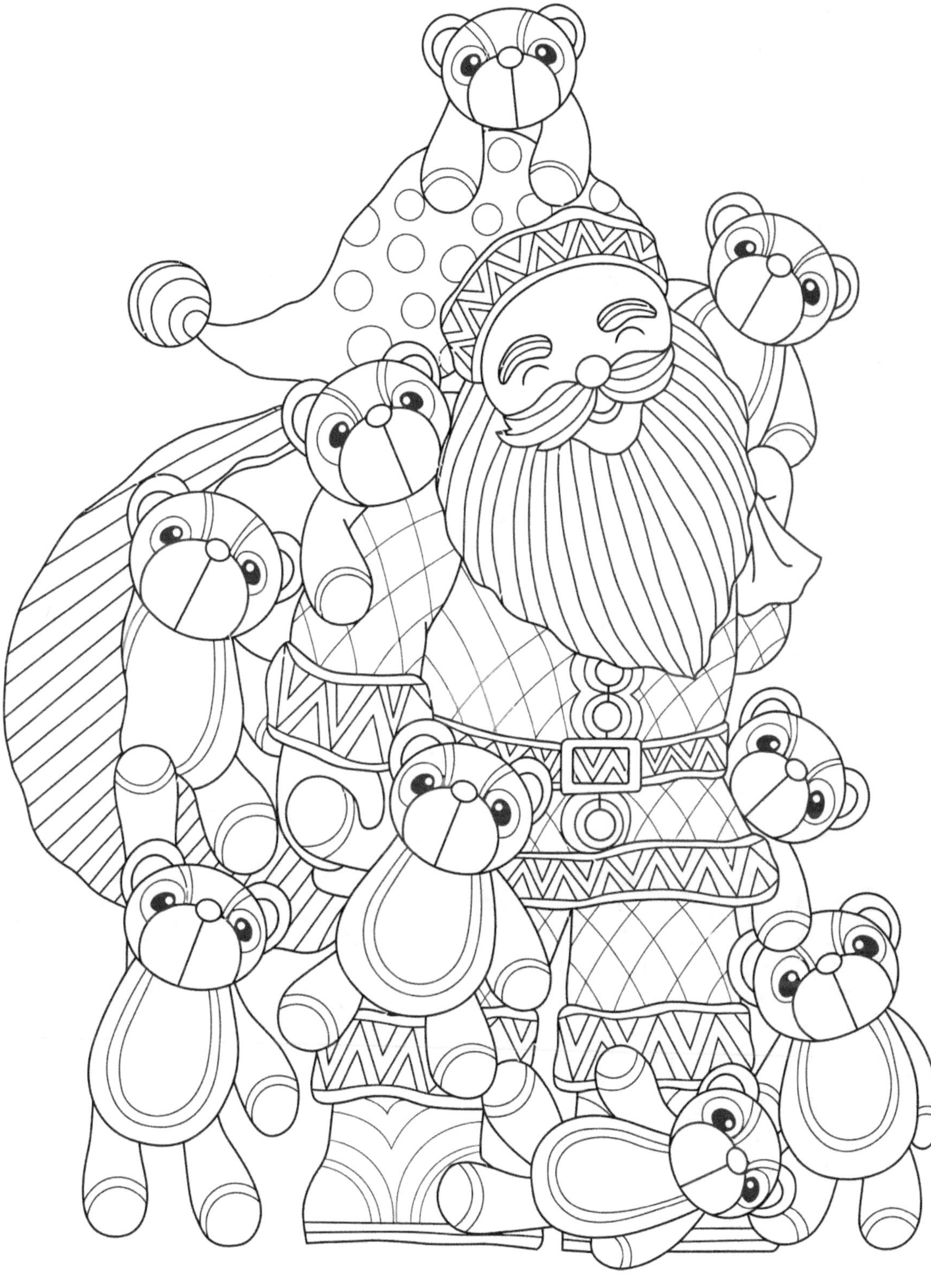

www.ingramcontent.com/pod-product-compliance
Lightning Source LLC
Chambersburg PA
CBHW081445220526
45466CB00008B/2518
* 9 7 9 8 5 7 5 8 8 5 6 0 3 *